THE INTERNATIONAL LAW OF COMMUNICATIONS

THE INTERNATIONAL LAW
OF COMMUNICATIONS

edited by

EDWARD McWHINNEY

A. W. SIJTHOFF, LEYDEN

OCEANA PUBLICATIONS INC., DOBBS FERRY, N.Y.

1971

K
.I 61
L415

ISBN 90 218 9011 9 Sijthoff

Library of Congress Catalog Card Number: 73-140557
© A. W. Sijthoff's Uitgeversmaatschappij, N.V. 1970

ACKNOWLEDGMENTS

The essays in this volume grew out of a special colloquium on the new international law of communications, with special reference to tele-communications and direct satellite broadcasting, held in the Institute of Air and Space Law at McGill University, Montreal, on May 25 and 26, 1970, in conjunction with the Annual Reunion of the Association des Auditeurs et Anciens Auditeurs de l'Académie de Droit International de la Haye. Some of the essays were presented for the colloquium and have since been revised for purposes of publication, while other essays have been specially prepared for the present volume.

The support of the Twentieth Century Fund, New York, in connection with the organization of the colloquium and the general preparation of the papers, is gratefully acknowledged. In particular, we wish to take note of the encouragement, advice and assistance generously given by M. J. Rossant, Director of the Fund, and also by various officers of the Fund, notably Miss Judi Seidel, Charles Pepper, Gordon Weil (now of Washington, D.C.) and Harold Goldberg. Translations into English of the original French texts of the papers prepared by Messrs. Errera and d'Arcy were made by Georges Thomson of Etrochey, Côte d'Or, France, currently a postgraduate student at McGill University, and by Sheila Macbrayne, Secretary of the Institute of Air and Space Law at McGill University. Assistance with the preparation of the material for publication was also given by Mr. E. A. Zussman-Ben-Yakir, also a post-graduate student at McGill University.

June 1, 1970

Edward McWhinney
Faculty of Law
McGill University
Montreal

CONTRIBUTORS

Chayes, Abram. Professor of Law, Harvard University, Cambridge, Massachusetts. Legal Adviser, U.S. Department of State, 1961-64.

d'Arcy, Jean. Director, Radio and Visual Services Division, Office of Public Information, United Nations, New York.

Elias, Hon. T. O. Attorney-General of Nigeria, Lagos. President, International Law Commission, United Nations.

Errera, Roger. Maître des requêtes au Conseil d'Etat, Paris. Chargé d'enseignement à la faculté de droit et des sciences économiques de l'université de Reims.

Hinchman, Walter R. Consultant on Domestic and International Communications, Boulder, Colorado.

Hondius, Frits W. Member of the Secretariat, The Council of Europe, Strasbourg.

Jacobson, Harold Karan. Professor of Political Science and Director, International Organization Program, University of Michigan, Ann Arbor.

Kopal, Vladimir. Senior Research Fellow, Institute of Law, Czechoslovak Academy of Sciences. Associate Professor, Charles University, Prague.

McWhinney, Edward. Q.C., Professor of Law, McGill University, Montreal. Director, Institute of Air and Space Law, Montreal.

Rao, K. Krishna. Additional Secretary and Legal Adviser, Ministry of External Affairs, Government of India, New Delhi.

Valladao, Hon. Haroldo. Professor of Law at the Catholic and Federal Universities of Rio de Janeiro. Formerly Attorney-General of Brazil.

7

CONTRIBUTORS

TABLE OF CONTENTS

Chapter 1

THE DEVELOPMENT OF AN INTERNATIONAL LAW OF COMMUNICATIONS

by *Edward McWhinney,* Montreal

An international law of communications that will be both rational and effective as law-in-action in an era where science and technology constantly move in advance of the society that they are supposed to serve may reasonably be expected to accord with the following policy objectives. *First,* the maintenance of a continuing high rate of scientific and general technological innovation and growth, without too many artificial hindrances and encumbrances imposed by *a priori* constitutional-institutional prescriptions at the international organizational level. *Second,* as low as possible a capital investment or capital commitment for the individual participants (whether public [government] or private organizations) consistent with the maintenance of scientific and technological progress. *Third,* as wide as possible a political commitment to the principle of free dissemination of information and ideas, without artificial restrictions or barriers imposed solely on account of national boundaries; for without such a commitment the central principle of communications as a social medium would seem to be vitiated.

If we look at the international law of communications that has in fact developed to date we can hardly avoid noting that, by and large, it has been refreshingly free from the dead-hand control of "institution-itis"—a concept which may be defined as the pursuit of abstract institutional forms and patterns for their own sake and at the expense of the concrete social purposes and objectives for which those institutions are designed and which alone give them their meaning and *raison d'être.* It may be suggested, in fact, that the pursuit of the organizational blueprint and the preoccupation with constitutional drafting, as such, at the expense of a functional, problem-solving orientation, accounts for the *malaise* of many contemporary international organizations, particularly at the U.N. specialized agency level. Be that as it may, the existing international law of communications is the product, essentially, of pragmatic initiative empirically applied in case-by-case development of principle. This origin accounts in considerable measure for the fact that there is, as yet, no single, overarching body of law, no one legally paramount international organization having jurisdiction over communications, no single code of principles or similar comprehensive enactment of positive law rules. What we have is rather a congeries of international law categories. Some of the rules derive from attempts at universal, law-making conventions or treaties in particular areas, the phrasing of these treaties usually attaining a fairly high level of generality and abstraction; some of them proceed from relatively specific or immediate bilateral agreements, accords or *ad hoc* contracts between two or more countries, usually on a regional grouping basis; some have been induced by analogy from the general, customary rules of international law in other, supposedly cognate areas; some stem from various institutional competences, whether of long standing and created for rather different or more general purposes, or else created more or less *ad hoc* in response to the pressing and immediate problems of the new telecommunications satellites.

An example of the first source of international law rules, in the category of high-level, norm-making ventures, is the Space Treaty of 1967, which, in its opening article, enunciates the general principle that the exploration and use of outer space shall be "carried out for the benefit and in the interests of all countries, irrespective of their degree of economic or scientific development," and that outer space shall be "the province of all mankind." Article 2 of the Treaty reaffirms this principle, declaring outer space to be "not subject to national appropriation by claim of sovereignty, by means of use or occupation, or by any other means." Beyond this the Treaty, both in its Preamble and specifically in Article 3, seeks to establish a general duty of "international cooperation" in the exploration and use of outer space.

The main weaknesses of the Treaty of 1967 are, of course, its very generality and its failure to include concrete operational rules, though these very limitations no doubt account for the relative ease and near unanimity with which the Treaty was accepted. Some parts of the Treaty—for example Article 5, concerning the rendering of assistance to astronauts in the event of accident, distress, or emergency—have since been fleshed out by more specific and detailed, low-level provisions, such as those embodied in the Agreement of 1968 on the Rescue of Astronauts, the Return of Astronauts and the Return of Objects Launched into Outer Space. By and large, however, the miltilateral treaty-based approach to international law-making has produced very few concrete, operational rules for the international law of communications, particularly in regard to the new science of television broadcasting from telecommunications satellites. The pronouncements in the

12

Space Treaty of 1967 remain, rather, as peripheral principles guiding perhaps, though not specifically restricting, the growth of detailed rules through such other means as international custom or *ad hoc* agreements between two or more countries.

The Space Treaty of 1967 has, perhaps, prevented a space race comparable to the grab for colonies by the European imperial powers and the nineteenth century staking out of spheres of political influence and sovereignty in Asia and Africa.

The Space Treaty does not, however, seem to have discouraged the desires of nations for ownership of "national" satellites. This attitude is analogous to the insistence of many newly independent ex-colonial countries on making the essentially prestige-seeking investment in a nationally operated international airline which they could ill afford to operate or even to maintain in continuing effective service. It is probably supported by bad fact-finding, stemming from a lack of technical sophistication on the part of national policy-makers and in particular from the old technical notion, now seemingly exploded, that only a finite number of "parking spaces" or orbital slots are available for satellites in outer space. A country may obtain all the benefits of a distinctive "national" satellite—apart, that is, from the mere gratification of national pride—more easily, more continuously, and certainly more cheaply through cooperation in more comprehensive regionally based or international satellite systems. The purchase through commercial contract or bilateral accord or treaty of an indefeasible right of use of, and access to, a shared satellite seems, in any case, in terms of comtemporary international legal science, more sophisticated than the old-fashioned, essentially nineteenth century, private-property-law-based national "ownership" of the particular hardware comprising a particular satellite in space. National ownership of particular hardware in outer space may not even be very realistic nationalism. As matters now stand, a nation can have its "national" satellite launched into orbit only by special contract with one of the two main consortium organizations, either the American-dominated or the Soviet-dominated one; and in the event of the temporary malfunctioning of that hardware in outer space, the nation would have to borrow equivalent facilities, again by special contract, from the satellites of one or the other of the two international consortium organizations.

The most fruitful developments in what we might call the "new" international law of communications have, in fact, proceeded via the contractual method—bilateral or limited multi-national, regional accords. The participants in this international law-making process are countries that on the whole share a rather high level of technical and scientific expertise as well as common cultural and social values. These similarities have held political conflicts and differences to a minimun, allowing the countries concerned to concentrate on the development of communications in their common interests and according to ordinary principles of business efficacy and scientific advancement, rather than on considerations of military or ideological advantage.

The most successful example of this essentially pragmatic, empirical approach to international law-making in the new communications field is the presently Western-controlled and essentially United States-dominated Intelsat (International Telecommunications Satellite Consortium). Candor requires it to be conceded that Intelsat's extraordinary progress in the field of telecommunications satellites in recent years, combining high scientific advances with unexpectedly low financial costs, has been largely the product of United States technological and managerial skill. Without this distinctively American contribution it would be hardly possible to talk seriously today about achieving a global system of telecommunications satellites.

The main contemporary criticisms of Intelsat, giving rise to the present discussions of its political and institutional restructuring, do not concern technical performance but an alleged lack of genuinely international character, due to the substantially U.S.-based control of its internal voting and decision-making powers, and to the U.S. monopoly of its managerial functions. The grounds for these objections are that because it supplied 53 per cent investment in the Intelsat system, the United States has 53 per cent of the voting power, not enough to make its own proposals prevail but enough to veto the proposals of others; and second, the conflict of interest inherent in the triple role of one United States government agency, Comsat, as a U.S. internal, domestic common carrier for profit; as the U.S. national representative to Intelsat; and as the general managerial authority within Intelsat.

Of these two issues, United States' voting power and control is the more serious. The United States government itself recognizes Comsat's managerial role with Intelsat as necessarily temporary and transitional; at the outset, all the Intelsat members accepted the necessity of giving Comsat managerial responsibility because in the early years of development of telecommunications satellites, Intelsat members other than the United States lacked comparable technological expertise.

14

The question of U.S. voting power, on the other hand, raises the politically sensitive and significant issue of weighted voting versus the one man (literally, one state)-one vote principle. Weighted voting is not by any means unheard of in contemporary (post-world War II) international organization. In fact, current trends in the constitutionalism of international organization may run against the overly literal pursuit of the one state-one vote principle, in reaction to some of the political excesses thought by many countries to be inherent in recent majority-imposed resolutions in the United Nations General Assembly, on some important international issues. Certainly, those international organizations whose political survival depends on the continuing good will and (more important perhaps) capital financing of the big powers— the International Monetary Fund and the United Nations Conference on Trade and Development, for example, and even the International Coffee Agreement—-have perforce abandoned the one state-one vote principle in favor of a politically more realistic distribution of voting power that will be proportional or somehow related to a particular country's expected capital contribution, or to the general economic and financial support and underwriting which it is to provide.

Rigid application of the one state-one vote system to Intelsat would, in theory, make it a more "democratic" international control organization, but surely also an intellectually and scientifically more sterile one if, for example, as a direct political consequence, the big powers with the technological know-how and the concomitant capital support should, as a result, decide to devote their main scientific and commercial energies to their own domestic telecommunications systems, possibly accompanied by direct bilateral agreements with other countries or groups of countries with a parallel advanced tecnological base. The logic of political events seems, in fact to suggest both retention of the weighted voting principle and diminution of the present 53 per cent voting power of the United States—a situation that one understands that the United States itself is perfectly willing to live with now.

The most serious limitation on Intelsat's "representative" character—from the political, if not the technical viewpoint—is not its weighted voting system but the fact that its membership represents, among the advanced technological societies, only the West and Western-leaning countries. The Soviet Union and the Soviet bloc countries in Eastern Europe are notably absent; as of course (though its telecommunications technology is, by comparison, much less advanced) is Communist China.

Of course, an effective, integrated world system of telecommunications satellites can function, under the aegis of Intelsat, without the Soviet Union and its own special Intersputnik organization covering its Eastern European associates. Yet scientific and technical cooperation between the United States and the leading Intelsat countries on the one hand, and the Soviet Union and the Intersputnik countries on the other, is clearly more desirable than cutthroat competition and mutual frustration between the two groups.

If the Soviet Union should be disposed to bid to join Intelsat, internal constitutional and structural changes within Intelsat would almost certainly follow, doing much to meet some of the current (essentially Western-based) criticisms of Intelsat's main organizational features. In particular, some degree of special voting powers in Intelsat for the Soviet Union (perhaps on the UNCTAD model, approaching though not exceeding those of the United States), automatically reducing the voting power of the United States below 50 per cent, seems inevitable. Any such measure would almost certainly be followed by some substantial modifications of Comsat's managerial functions to resolve the claimed "conflict of interest" in Comsat's role—assuming, of course, that such modifications should not already have been effectuated by that time.

If a Soviet Union bid to join Intelsat were favorably received, it would undoubtedly act as a sort of catalyst for far-reaching internal structural changes within Intelsat. It would also introduce a degree of political equilibrium into Intelsat, paralleling the balance of power and tacit understanding that have characterized other important areas of Soviet-Western interbloc relations in the era of the political *détente*. What is important, however, is the principle of Soviet-Western understanding in the telecommunications field, not the particular institutional form or modalities that embody this principle. Remembering the progress from essentially negative and hostile East-West "coexistence" in the very early years of the *détente* to some far more affirmative and concrete exercises in active East-West cooperation in more recent years, we need not necessarily give much concern to the question of whether such East-West cooperation in the field of telecommunication satellites should take the form of an actual Soviet bid to join Intelsat, generating a search within Intelsat for new constitutional formulae and international organizational solutions, or simply of direct *ad hoc* dealings between the Soviet Union and the West, limited to particular and immediate problems. The latter approach would be far more mod-

16

est, looking to bilateral, contractual-type dealings and arrangements, perhaps linking Intelsat and Intersputnik through conventional private-law-style arrangements. In the long run, however, if the experience of the International Law Association during the early 1960's in the "coexistence" debate between Soviet bloc and Western jurists is any example, we are likely to achieve far more results through a series of concrete and specific, relatively low-level, contractual relationships than through a search for holistic solutions involving the establishment of overarching constitutional-institutional patterns. Certainly the success of the very concrete, joint Soviet-French television program transmission exercises in recent months suggests once again that in areas involving high technical and scientific competence or expertise, two technologically sophisticated organizations located in different countries can work together effectively in their common interest despite ideological differences between the two countries.

A related institutional-organizational question concerns the distinction, well known to administrative lawyers, between managerial and regulatory activities. Intelsat has been concerned primarily with the former. Should such questions as registration and coordination of orbital patterns of telecommunication satellites, as well as control of program content and quality, also be left to Intelsat and complementary "regional" organizations like Intersputnik? Or should they be entrusted to some entirely separate and autonomous organization with more specialized responsibilities and expertise in regulatory activities involving communications? Some aspects of the regulatory problem such as the need, if any, for control of program content and quality, may perhaps have been exaggerated. Jean d'Arcy has addressed himself to the fears that development of direct satellite television broadcasting into home receivers may result in a 1984-type "thought control". He points out that in an earlier era, similar prophesies concerning radio as "thought control" or propaganda medium were widely exaggerated, and this during the height of the Cold War era. The problem does exist, of course. In September 1969, at an international scientific conference jointly sponsored by the Carnegie Endowment for International Peace and the Twentieth Century Fund, a Soviet jurist with a sense of humor, Dr. Gennady Zhukov, pointed out that while the direct satellite transmission of a bullfight actually taking place in a Spanish arena might be viewed as a cultural enrichment by television viewers in Mexico the same program at the same time might be seen by viewers in India as an affront or harm to group religious feelings. And Dr. Zhukov offered this example to

17

illustrate the need for some sort of preliminary agreement on program content and norms before we reach the era of direct television transmission by satellites into home receivers. To this I should add the Indian delegate, to whom, among others, Dr. Zhukov had directed his remarks, at once pointed out that the problem could of course be exaggerated, and that Indians had already learned to live with direct radio broadcasts from neighboring countries even on issues as politically sensitive as the India-Pakistan dispute over Kashmir.

If pressures for regulatory controls in this particular area are successful politically, they will probably take the form of some sort of general, multilateral international convention establishing general norms, though not necessarily with any very concrete institutional machinery for their application. The other, "quieter" forms of regulatory activity still remain, of course, and many existing international institutional organizations are available as candidates for the job of international control agency. Many United Nations specialized agencies —the International Civil Aviation Organization, the World Meteorological Organization, even UNESCO—hit some aspect or other of telecommunications. Moreover, the United Nations General Assembly's special Committee on the Peaceful Uses of Outer Space has already performed outstanding work in the progressive development of the international law of outer space; but its acceptance by the big powers may be handicapped by the asserted "politicization" in recent years of the United Nations General Assembly as a whole.

There remains, of course, the oldest of all the United Nations specialized agencies, the International Telecommunication Union (ITU), founded in 1865. ITU has the immediate advantage of near-universal membership. But in terms of the constitutional law of international organization, ITU is somewhat underdeveloped, and may in any case be handicapped by the narrowly technical (posts and telegraphs) character of most of the national delegations taking part in its proceedings. Without some radical change in the composition of ITU's decision-making and managerial personnel, and without some radical restructuring of its basic constitutional powers and internal organization, ITU could probably not assume major responsibilities in the new field of telecommunications satellites without impairing its existing specialized competence or political usefulness in its present somewhat limited and modest functions. Harold Jacobson has pointed, in particular, to the limitations on decision-making imposed by ITU's internal structure, which is conventional or treaty-based, in the older style, rather than charter or con-

18

stitution-based as the newer United Nations specialized agencies are. The members of a charter-based international organization agree to a basic constitution which includes fairly elaborate and stringent procedures for amendment, thus ensuring a certain administrative stability and continuity in decision-making processes. By contrast, at each ITU Plenipotentiary Conference, the entire Telecommunication Convention is in theory open to revision, and that by simple majority vote.

Nevertheless, it does seem reasonable to believe that institutional developments in the "regulatory" aspects of telecommunications will take place outside Intelsat, either building on other, existing international bodies that are at present peripheral to the telecommunications satellites field, or giving rise to new international committees or similar bodies, *ad hoc*.

For all the foregoing reasons, the new international law of communications is not likely to follow any one tidy, well-planned course of development and law-making but rather to proceed from a variety of different sources, pragmatically and often *ad hoc*. Again, we are not likely, in the immediate future, to have any one, universal institutional agency exercising a monopoly of decision-making power and control over telecommunications, but rather a plurality of organizations and agencies, some within the United Nations itself, some intergovernmental and regionally based, and some international but private and non-governmental. Frank acknowledgment of this prospect is certainly not counsel of despair. The international organization of telecommunications is likely to be, in fact, analogous to that of international civil aviation, where the control and authority pattern is established by one extremely general international convention, the Chicago Convention of 1944, postulating high-level policy norms; a number of more detailed, ancillary international conventions hitting fairly specific air law problems only; an international intergovernmental organization, ICAO, representing most, but not all, of the major governments of the world; an international private organization, IATA, representing most, but not all, of the major civil airline companies of the world, both private and governmental; a very great number of bilateral treaties or particular accords concluded between specific countries within the general framework of the Chicago Convention, covering detailed issues of landing rights, traffic rights, and the like; plus a series of international private law, contractual type, traffic conference agreements, covering the crucial issues of fares and related problems and apparently depending for their legal efficacy in the strict sense upon international

19

private law, plus any additional public law support accorded to them, by legal indirection as it were, through reference back to the welter of bilateral treaties concluded between the main countries of the world. In fact, the internal cohesion and cooperation within the airline industry is far more dependent upon mutuality and reciprocity of interest among the major airlines and their supporting governments than on any formal legal sanctions.

The success that international civil aviation has displayed in the past half-century, combining a very high rate of scientific and technical progress with continuing economic growth, has certainly in no way been arrested or impeded by the highly heterogeneous, pluralistic character of its institutional organization at the international level and by the effective allocation or division of law-making competence among a number of parallel and complementary but not competing authorities. This pluralism seems in fact to have encouraged a high degree of regional experimentation in the common interest, without creating too many problems of coordination of different regional policies at the center. At the conference in Chicago that preceded the adoption of the Chicago Convention of 1944, the United States had pressed initially for a central principle of the freedom of the air, to be concretized in one overarching body of international law principles and to be institutionalized in the one paramount international agency. When these hopes were not realized, the United States delegation wisely settled for something less.

The resulting control authority may seem unnecessarily complex and untidy in an international administrative law sense, but it does work, and indeed it seems to work very much better than do, for example, some of the United Nations specialized agencies that have far tidier constitutional charters and institutional blueprints.

The likelihood is, then, that we may have a somewhat similar pattern of development for the new international law of communications—variegated and pluralistic, developing in a rather pragmatic, empirical, problem-oriented, step-by-step way. This approach to international law-making in the new communications field may not satisfy some of the constitutional theorists of international organization, but it seems more likely to continue to combine maximum scientific progress with a high rate of technological and industrial expansion and low overall commercial costs than the other, essentially *a priori,* abstract approach to the development of an international law of communications.

Chapter 2

THE TECHNOLOGICAL ENVIRONMENT FOR INTER-NATIONAL COMMUNICATIONS LAW

by *Walter R. Hinchman,* Boulder, Colorado

The objective of this paper is to highlight those technological consider-ations which have been of primary importance in the past development of international communications law, as well as those which are likely to affect future developments. The two foci of this examination are sys-tem design and operation and the use and management of the radio spectrum resource.

Rather than try to provide encyclopedic coverage of all technologi-cal considerations, the paper will treat some key developments and basic characteristics of telecommunications facilities in considerable depth, relating each to important policy and institutional issues either actual or potential.

Communications satellite technology is the aspect of telecommuni-cations that promises to have the greatest impact on future international operations and use of the radio spectrum resource. The paper therefore discusses other technologies only in terms of their past impact and like-lihood of significant future developments.

THE PRE-SATELLITE ERA

Technology and system characteristics

The earliest means of telecommunication transmission was the over-land telegraph cable, invented by Samuel F.B. Morse in 1844. During the next hundred years, it was followed by submarine telegraph cables, overland telephone lines, high-frequency radio transmission subma-rine telephone cables, microwave radio relay links, and coaxial tele-phone and telegraph cables for both overland and undersea use. Each of these transmission modes represented a significant improvement over previous modes in either quality and reliability of service or channel capacity and per-circuit cost. At the same time, each represented but an extension of a particular type of transmission capability. All might be characterized as *single-route, fixed-capacity* transmission links. That is, a particular set of transmission facilities is capable of linking together only two points on the earth's surface (single route), and the message-carrying capacity of this link, determined by its particular design parameters, is fixed and cannot be reallocated to or shared with other routes.

Some of the principal characteristics of single-route, fixed-capacity transmission facilities are worthy of note, for they have profoundly affected the development of institutions and the formulation of policy dealing with both domestic and international telecommunications. First, the cost of such facilities is typically a direct function of distance along the earth's surface; thus it is desirable to minimize the total length of transmission links used. Second, the cost per circuit of such facilities tends to decrease with increasing number of circuits per link; thus it is desirable to amalgamate all the traffic destined to or from a sizable area for transmission over a few high-capacity links rather than many low-capacity links. Also, high-capacity facilities shared by many customers with random needs can be used much more efficiently than can multiple low-capacity facilities.

These characteristics lead to an optimum configuration for terrestrial communication services which consists of a hierarchy of transmission links of ever-increasing capacity, interconnected via intermediate switching and routing facilities, generally referred to as a communications network or grid. For international communications, this network typically culminates in from one to a very few international routing centers for each nation, which are then interconnected via either HF (high-frequency) radio (if traffic volume over a particular route is very low), microwave radio relay (if volume is high between adjacent nations), or submarine cable (if volume is high between particular regions on separate continents).

The advent of radio communication technology in the early 1900's did bring some different capabilities to the telecommunications field (e.g., the ability to "broadcast" messages simultaneously to many receivers over a sizable area, and the ability to establish different transmission links at different times via a single set of HF radio equipment). However, the limited coverage and capacity of these early radio systems foreclosed any possibility of utilizing such capabilities for large-scale two-way telecommunication services.

The technical and economic characteristics of two-way telecommunication systems employing single-route fixed-capacity links have per-

22

mitted the adoption of a unilateral approach to domestic telecommunications and a bilateral approach to international telecommunication arrangements. This result was natural because, given the hierarchical network structure, typically only one or two parties need be directly involved in the establishment, financing and operation of such facilities.

Radio resource use and management

Electromagnetic radiation (radio waves) is a form of energy comparable to radiant heat and light and capable of traveling freely through space, atmospheric gases, etc., without any physical interconnecting link. It can be used to carry information over distance. (Radio waves oscillate at different rates of speed [frequencies], and one of the several characteristics by which one radio wave may be distinguished from another is the frequency of its oscillation. Other distinguishing features are polarization, intensity, time of existence, direction of propagation, occupied space and "modulation," or manner in which information is superimposed on the frequency, time and intensity characteristics.)

The first radio waves generated by man oscillated at rates that are now considered relatively slow (e.g., in the 0 to 30 million cycles per second [30 MHz] range). At the time, however, this frequency range was considered quite extensive.

One of the first discoveries concerning radio transmission was that the early radio receivers could not distinguish between two radio waves oscillating at the same frequency. To prevent "interference" between radio signals used for different purposes each radio system came to employ a different set of oscillation frequencies; this restriction imposed little inhibition on early radio system development, as the range of frequencies in relation to demand was virtually unlimited.

Another early discovery was that the radio energy being utilized (i.e., radio waves in the 0-30 MHz range) traveled around the globe with only modest reduction in intensity, being sustained by reflection from the earth's ionosphere and conduction along the earth's surface. This characteristic made global telecommunication possible, but it also meant that any nation's use of radio, in particular its use of waves oscillating at certain frequencies, inevitably affected other nations' use of radio, at least of those frequencies.

Radio usage grew rapidly in the early 1900's, thanks to the economic advantage over wire and cable resulting from the ability of radio waves to traverse space and inhospitable terrain without physical interconnec-

23

tions. This growth was accompanied by a growing need to prevent interference, which eventually gave rise to "frequency management," i.e. administrative procedures by which radio systems and services were authorized to employ specific oscillation frequencies. Frequency management initially took the form of international agreements on coordination of radio system development. The long-range nature of the HF transmission mode made such coordination necessary and the coordination of radio operating frequencies presented the clearest means of preventing harmful interference in the 0 to 30 MHz frequency range. The International Radio Telegraph Union was established as the agency of international coordination in the selection of non-interfering operating frequencies for radio systems; the International Telecommunication Union inherited this function after radio and telegraph coordinating activities were merged in 1932. This organization allocates particular ranges of permissible operating frequencies to specific classes of service; it also registers specific frequency usage by individual nations, alerting other nations to employ different frequencies; and it develops voluntary technical standards and operating practices for the telecommunications systems of its members. Most of the advanced nations interested in using radio systems have also established their own national frequency management authorities, operated along similar lines. These operating principles of these agencies have changed relatively little since they were established, despite intervening developments which have altered the meaning and purpose of frequency management.

The technological environment in which radio frequency management operates began to change rather significantly with the advant of VHF (30-300 MHz) and UHF (300-3,000 MHz) transmission capability in the 1930's and continued to change markedly with the development of higher frequency (microwave, millimeterwave, laser) capabilities during the 1950's and 1960's. Since radio energy at frequencies much above 30 MHz is neither reflected by the ionosphere nor conducted effectively by the earth's surface, the range of operations and danger of interference at these frequencies is limited to the horizon or modest extensions beyond; global coordination of, or uniformity in, the use of such frequencies is thus unnecessary. Furthermore, the art of modulation, detection, and coding of information carried by these signals has advanced to the stage where operating frequencies even within a given area can be shared in many instances without interference; thus the principle that different systems must use different frequencies is no longer valid. Moreover, radiation at very high frequencies can be focused

24

into narrow beams. It can also be effectively polarized (i.e. have its electric and magnetic fields oriented in particular directions); focus and polarization are two more features that can distinguish one radio wave from another even when both possess identical frequency characteristics and exist within the same area.

Some recognition of deficiencies in the "frequency" approach to radio resource management during the past two or three decades has led to a gradual breakdown of the global uniformity in frequency usage and technical standards. However, this recognition has not given rise to a new approach; it has merely produced inconsistency in frequency allocations within different regions. Management within each region has retained its frequency orientation and generally views decisions on the uses of frequencies within a particular region for particular services as a subject for global determination.

In summary, the early development of telecommunication services was firmly based on the characteristics of dedicated, single-route transmission facilities and HF radio which led to national sovereignty in the provision of domestic services, bilateral arrangements for international services and global, multilateral management of the radio resource through the allocation and registration of particular operating frequencies for particular radio services, although these procedures have been modified somewhat in recent years for radio systems operating above the HF range.

THE EARLY SATELLITE ERA

The advent of communication satellite technology in the early 1960's rendered some of the basic principles of communication system design and operation obsolete. White the frequent characterization of satellites as nothing more than radio relay stations in the sky is fundamentally correct, it is also an oversimplification which tends to mask some major differences in the operational capabilities of satellite and terrestrial systems. Satellite communication facilities (both earth and space stations) are inherently capable of serving multiple routes through a single facility, and of reallocating channel capacity flexibility among these routes—capabilities not enjoyed by terrestrial facilities. The operational and economic significance of this *multiple-route, allocable-capacity* capability, yet to be fully utilized, will be discussed in some detail following a brief review of satellite developments to date.

25

Initially, it was thought by many that satellite communications would be achieved through low-altitude, random-orbit (i.e., constantly moving) satellites. The Telstar experiment conducted by the American Telephone and Telegraph Company was the culmination of this particular approach. This type of system would have required thirty to forty satellites for full global coverage, each of which would be used at different times by different sets of earth stations around the world. Each earth station would require multiple, fully tracking antennas in order to establish communication links through successive satellites as they came into view while maintaining links through satellites passing from view. To establish a multiplicity of links among many nations would have required complex scheduling of satellites, on-board radio repeaters, and earth stations.

The complexity and cost envisaged for such a system, plus the fact that any one satellite would be of use to a particular nation for only a small percentage of time, led to the conclusion that the financing and use of a communication satellite system would require global participation. Accordingly, the International Telecommunications Satellite Consortium (Intelsat) was formed to develop a single global system for international satellite communications.

Contrary to expectations, Intelsat did not adopt the random orbit satellite configuration, which thus became the first major discard of the communications satellite era. It was supplanted by a geostationary satellite system following the successful emplacement into earth synchronous orbit of Syncom II, a satellite designed and built by the Hughes Aircraft Company and launched by the American National Aeronautics and Space Administration in 1963. This event actually predated signing of the Intelsat interim agreements but had little impact on the nature of those agreements. It has had and will continue to have a profound impact on the development of satellite technology, operations and economics.

Initially, a geostationary satellite system seemed preferable to a random-orbit satellite system mainly because it required fewer satellites for full global coverage and reduced the complexity and scheduling problems of earth stations. Geostationary satellites travel in an orbit directly above the equator at a speed that is synchronized with the earth's rotation so that they appear to occupy fixed positions relative to the earth's surface. Because each geostationary satellite is "visible from roughly 40 per cent of the earth's surface, as few as three such satellites properly spaced can "cover" the entire surface of the earth, exclusive of extreme northern and southern latitudes; and a particular set of earth stations can view a specific satellite and schedule the use of its radio repeaters on a permanent basis without need for extensive tracking or complex scheduling arrangements. Since these characteristics were readily convertible into cost savings, Intelsat adopted the geostationary configuration beginning with the Intelsat I satellite launched in 1965.

Other operational advantages of the geostationary configuration have emerged over the past several years, and some anticipated problems have proven illusory. It soon became apparent that the fixed location and orientation of such satellites in relation to the earth's surface would permit the use of directive (focused) satellite antennas, capable of producing more powerful illumination of the earth's surface from the limited power generation capability available; such antenna directivity would not have been useful with continuously orbiting, unoriented satellites. Also, the geostationary configuration rendered frequency sharing between earth stations and terrestrial radio relay stations much more feasible, since only one or at most a few specific antenna pointing angles need be cleared from potential interference. The major disadvantage anticipated, i.e., the longer time delay and potentially displeasing echo effects resulting from the very high altitude of geostationary satellites, have produced little degradation for one-hop satellite links, and may even be acceptable for two-hop links as well. The geostationary configuration thus appears firmly established as the optimum means for providing most satellite communications services, though random orbit configurations may be utilized for specialized services (e.g., meteorological and navigational satellites, etc.).

In the final analysis, the use made of any communication mode will depend on its superiority to some alternative mode of providing a desired service. To date, the communication satellite has proven more economical than its competition, undersea cable, for long transoceanic links, the advantage increasing with the distance to be covered and the sparseness of routes (low traffic volume). This advantage lies in the satellite's *multiple-route* as opposed to *single-route* capabilities. Since terrestrial interconnecting links must traverse a specific path along the earth's surface, their cost increases with the distance between the points they connect. Each such link typically interconnects but two points. The traffic volume between those two points serves to justify the costs of the link and the cost per circuit decreases as the number of circuits increases. Therefore only the anticipation of heavy traffic can justify the

27

expense of long interconnecting links.

Within the coverage area of a given satellite, the basic cost of a communications link between it and an earth station is essentially the earth station cost, which is nearly uniform for all earth stations. Thus the basic cost of a link (not a circuit) between two earth stations via satellite is largely independent of the *distance* separating them. Furthermore, since a single earth station may simultaneously link with many other stations via the same satellite relay, the basic cost *per route* decreases as the number of routes per station increases. Of course certain other variable costs for both satellites and earth stations do increase in direct proportion to the number of routes served, but they have a much smaller effect on the total costs because they are not duplicated many times along the transmission path of a satellite system as they are in terrestrial systems.

To determine total costs of satellite service, one must add to these basic costs the per-circuit cost of both satellite and earth station facilities. Since both these facilities serve multiple routes, the volume of traffic over a given route has little effect on per-circuit costs. The *total* volume of traffic through each facility (satellite or earth station), like that of terrestrial systems, reduces per-circuit costs as the number of circuits increases. Thus, per-circuit costs of satellite interconnection within a given coverage zone are largely independent of the number of routes or indivual route traffic volume but inversely proportional to the total traffic volume over all routes served.

Thus satellites have a cost advantage in providing long, low-traffic routes, particularly when several such routes are served via a single satellite-earth station combination; while terrestrial facilities will be most competitive over shorter routes having high traffic volumes, particularly where only one route is required from a given location.

The early evolution of satellite communications has in general followed that principle. Transoceanic communications between developed and developing nations, and among developing nations both characteristically involving low-volume, multiple-route services, have benefited significantly from satellite development. On the other hand, proponents of undersea cables have successfully defended continued deployment of such facilities on shorter, high-volume routes between developed nations, though much of the rationale here has centered on redundancy in transmission modes rather than economic advantage.

28

The characteristics of early satellite systems have brought about further reappraisals of the basic premises of radio resource use and management; even more sweeping changes may be forecast for the future.

The advent of communication satellite technology in the early 1960's brought the realization that the radio frequency range in which such services could best be developed (between about 1,000 and 10,000 MHz) was already allocated among, and heavily used by, various terrestrial radio services. To have provided exclusive frequency allocations of the large bandwidth needed for satellite services would thus have necessitated either reallocation from terrestrial services or allocation of bands above 10,000 MHz which, for technical, operational and economic reasons, were much less desirable. The Space Extraodinary Administrative Radio Conference (EARC), convened in 1963 by ITU to consider this problem, concluded with the recognition that satellite and certain terrestrial systems could operate at the same frequencies simultaneously without mutual interference, since the propagation paths would be significantly different. Specifically, it was determined that microwave radio relay services (which employ narrow-beam transmission along fixed routes paralleling the earth's surface) and satellite services (whose transmission paths extend outward from the earth's surface) could avoid harmful mutual interference through coordination of the siting and design parameters of their systems. This case was the first in which two different classes of service were authorized simultaneous use of common operating frequencies in a common area, and it represents a significant precedent for future radio resource management. To date, this approach has been successful; despite dire forecasts of serious interference problems no instances of such interference have been reported.

During this formative period of satellite development, there has likewise been no difficulty in accommodating prospective uses within the finite capacity of the allocated radio frequency spectrum and the geostationary orbital space available. The use of narrow-beam radiation along different transmission paths not only reduces the danger of interference between satellite and terrestrial systems but also prevents harmful interference between satellite systems if the satellites are adequately separated along the geostationary orbit. Intelsat has thus far required relatively few satellites (from one to three per ocean basin) to handle international traffic, and the one to three degree separation feasible with Intelsat's large eighty-five foot diameter earth stations would permit

29

many more such satellites to be emplaced. However, growing interest in the use of satellites for domestic and regional services has created considerable fear that the frequency spectrum and/or the geostationary orbital arc will be inadequate to accommodate all such requirements. This concern has evoked different reactions from those involved. First, most competent radio engineers who have analyzed the situation conclude that the ability to accommodate future demands on the radio spectrum and orbit resource by satellite systems is virtually unlimited, and that fear of scarcity is thus unjustified. On the other hand, some frequency management authorities and proponents of the "single global system" concept contend that the threat of scarcity is serious and that the best way to utilize the available capacity is through a single, unified global system or at most a select, coordinated group of regional systems. Meanwhile developing nations, foreseeing that satellites may be uniquely suited to their future communication needs and fearing that nations with more immediate access to this technology may "use up" the available spectrum and orbit capacity, have called for international allocation and assignment of this resource to protect their interests. The validity of these differing views will be evaluated in a subsequent section on future opportunities.

A final comment concerning the impact of early communication satellite development on radio resource use and management seems worthy of mention. As noted previously, the earlier advent of terrestrial radio systems employing frequencies above 30 MHz eventually brought the realization that many frequency management requirements were indeed regional in nature and that global uniformity in the allocation and technical standardization process was unnecessary throughout most of the radio frequency spectrum. However, early satellites which required these higher operating frequencies yet were technologically incapable of illuminating less than the entire exposed face of the earth, arrested that progress and led many to conclude that global unformity was still essential. This attitude was reflected in the allocations for satellite communications from the Space EARC of 1963; in the use of those allocations since that conference; and in tentative proposals submitted to the forthcoming 1971 World Administrative Radio Conference (WARC), which will consider further allocations for space services. The validity and potential consequences of this concept will also be evaluated in the following section.

30

The preceding sections have focused on what *has been* done and the concepts which have guided telecommunications development and radio resource management and use. This section will concentrate on what *could be* done if technical and economic considerations dominated future development in both these areas.

Technological developments

In attempting to project future technological developments and their impact, one is always at the mercy of one's initial assumptions. It is thus crucial that these be clearly stated as the basis of the projection. For example, some maintain that the technology for direct broadcast satellites is presently available, while others contend it is ten, fifteen or more years away. Both are in a sense correct within their particular framework of assumptions, yet the assertions themselves provide little guidance for policy or planning. The fact is, the basic technology for "direct" broadcast to modestly augmented home TV receivers *is* available today, according to certain definitions of the terms *basic technology* and *augmented*. Specifically, spacecraft of the Intelsat 4 and slightly larger size could generate enough power and support antennas large enough to "broadcast" one or more TV channels over a limited area, which could be received via antennas five to ten feet in diameter with solid-state preamplifiers, frequency translators, and modulation converters. Such "augmentation" might cost between $ 100 and $ 1,000, depending on quantity, available production skills, etc. On the other hand, without a commitment to direct satellite broadcasting strong enough to justify the cost of not only developing and building the satellite itself but also carrying out the ground system augmentation, it will probably take at least ten or fifteen years for such a capability to develop. The author believes that such a capability is five years away, not for lack of technology but because of uncertain economics and applications, programming limitations, and other non-technical factors. As for direct broadcasting to unaugmented home receivers, although it is said to be "possible" within ten to twenty years, it may never become a reality at all, again not for technological or even political reasons but simply because a more cost-effective solution will be found, probably involving transmission to augmented receivers capable of serving a small group of households, a school or a village complex.

31

Highly directive satellite antennas: Leaving aside such complex inter-disciplinary questions for the moment, probably the most significant technological development of the near future will be the use of stabilized, highly directive spacecraft antennas. While the Intelsat 3 and 4 series of satellites have made some use of such antennas, the tremendous "power" of these techniques is yet to be fully appreciated. In terms of individual system optimization, where this technique is operationally satisfactory (e.g., for domestic or regional services involving limited geographic areas) it can reduce the cost of satellite circuits by an order of magnitude (a 10 to 1 ratio). For example, the first geostationary satellites pumped their limited energy into a doughnut-shaped antenna radiation pattern some 20° by 360° in extent, of which the earth occupied but 17° by 17°. The resultant energy density (watts per square meter) at the earth's surface was but $17 \times 17/20 \times 360$, or 1/25 what it would have been had the antenna illuminated only the earth. Earth stations had to be twenty-five times more sensitive than would otherwise have been necessary to derive a given number of communications circuits from this satellite, and they were correspondingly more expensive. We now have 17° by 17° antenna beams and will soon have 4.5° by 4.5° antenna beams from Intelsat 4, all using the 4 and 6 GHz (gigahertz, or billion cycles per second) frequency bands. It is technologically possible to obtain beamwidths of 1° to 2°, covering an area smaller than a single state or province, using the 4 and 6 GHz frequency bands and available launch vehicles. In 1972-73, NASA will launch its ATS-F and G experimental satellites with unfurlable antennas of thirty feet in diameter, capable of providing 0.5° beamwidths at 4 or 6 GHz or less than 0.2° beamwidths at 15 GHz. Even with a 1° by 1° beamwidth, the energy density at the earth's surface from a given in-orbit power source can be increased by a factor of 7,200 relative to Syncom 2; alternatively, the in-orbit power can be divided among several such antenna beams, each providing a significant increase in energy density over any satellite to date. In either case, the cost per circuit of satellite communications can be driven downward markedly, either from reduction in earth station size, sensitivity and cost or from the derivation of more channels per satellite, or both. The implication for domestic and regional services is clear: satellite systems will become much more competitive with terrestrial alternatives as the coverage area per satellite beam is reduced. Note that this reduction in coverage does not automatically imply the loss of long-distance service via such satellites; a satellite using two or more narrow beams to illuminate separate areas provides all

32

the advantages cited, while still permitting long-distance interconnection between these areas (up to the satellite's limit of visibility) via interconnection between beams at the satellite.

Demand assignment of satellite channels: The next most significant development in satellite communications will be the ability to allocate satellite channel capacity flexibly and on demand among the multiple routes served. As noted earlier, because terrestrial multi-channel transmission facilities are inherently limited to single-route operation, channel capacity cannot be reallocated among routes. However, since traffic demand between any two points varies widely, efficient operation of transmission facilities requires some means of minimizing the amount of idle capacity. In terrestrial systems, the solution is the creation of a network of transmission facilities interconnected by switching and routing facilities so that traffic between any two points may be routed via several alternative transmission links; or, looked at in a different manner, each fixed-path, fixed-capacity transmission link may be used as part of the route between several different points. This solution requires, however, an extensive hierarchy of switching and routing facilities in addition to the basic transmission facilities, resulting in additional costs.

To date, satellites have been used merely to provide alternative transmission links among existing switching and routing centers. However, since a single satellite serves many earth stations and routes via a single, broadband radio repeater, the full satellite channel capacity is potentially available to each earth station or route. The channel capacity of a given satellite can therefore be allocated and reallocated among the many routes served according to their current traffic requirements. This reallocation does not require intermediate switching and routing facilities. It simply involves advising the respective earth stations which satellite channels to use for particular routes. It also requires flexible channel selection equipment for each earth station, but this flexibility can be achieved by a variety of techniques comparable to the multiplex techniques used to terminate any multi-channel transmission link, and may not be much more costly.

In short, contrary to some representations, satellites are not "just another transmission medium" but can substitute for both the transmission and the switching-routing facilities required in terrestrial networks. The basic technology for providing this demand-assigned channel usage is available, and several prototype systems have already been built. Where such techniques can effectively utilized they may result in significant cost savings relative to the normal network configuration.

Inter-satellite relay: One of the problems of planning satellite communication systems has been the limited capacity and/or visibility of an individual satellite. These limitations manifest themselves in various ways. Intelsat's primary concerns are the inability of a single satellite to handle all the "international" traffic within a given ocean basin, the inability of the minimum three-satellite global configuration to provide direct links both east and west from many nations, and the necessity of undesirable multiple-hop transmission or long surface links to reach many distant points. While the deployment of additional satellites could alleviate all these problems with present technology, the use of additional satellites would necessitate a multiplication of earth stations, and would create difficult problems of scheduling and organizing the routes to be served through this multiplicity of facilities.

Problems of the same sort arise with regard to domestic or regional satellite uses, with even greater complexity. The use of narrow-beam satellite antennas, so desirable as a means of increasing capacity and reducing costs within a limited area, could render satellite communications between areas served by different satellites more difficult. Also, the likelihood of much higher volumes of domestic and regional traffic means that each such system may itself require several satellites, producing the same problems of multiple earth stations and scheduling but in spades. Finally, heavy reliance on satellites systems for domestic and regional services may ultimately make it necessary for international communications via Intelsat satellites to use two-hop circuits, considered by many communicators undesirable for voice communications due to time-delay and echo effects.

These problems would indeed be serious if future satellite communication systems were to be mere replicas of existing systems. Fortunately, however, new stabilized satellite platforms to accommodate the directive antennas previously described provide solutions to these problems. Present technology makes it feasible—though not yet demonstrated—to install radio repeaters and directive antennas on satellites to provide *inter-satellite* relay links. Using extremely high frequencies with bandwidths capable of carrying the full channel capacity of many earth-space links, it will be possible to interconnect several satellites in space. As previously noted, satellites can increase the communications capacity obtainable from a given frequency allocation by sharing frequency

34

allocations with other satellites suitably separated along the orbit and serving the same or different geographic areas. When coupled with inter-satellite relay capability this multiplication of channel capacity does not require multiple earth stations at each location, since each earth station could obtain access to this total pool of satellite channels by linking to a single satellite. Inter-satellite relay can link a "visible" satellite to another satellite beyond the coverage area of the satellite being viewed. The inter-satellite relay can also permit transoceanic or "international" communication without multi-hop limitations, by linking either satellites serving different domestic/regional areas, or such satellites and transoceanic satellites where these are warranted. The coverage area and capacity of any transoceanic satellite system can also be extended through increased numbers of satellites using inter-satellite relay, again without requiring additional earth stations.

Lest this discussion raise the specter of the existence of exceedingly sophisticated and unreliable spacecraft containing in effect massive "switchboards in the sky," it should be noted that they involve the same demand-assignment techniques mentioned earlier, in which the earth station does the actual "switching" although in effect the satellite is the routing center. In other words, certain up-link and down-link channels in each satellite could be permanently connected to inter-satellite relay channels, with the earth stations involved in any particular inter-satellite route being advised which up- and down-link channels to use for their particular traffic requirement. In fact, these up- and down-link satellite channels could be permanently connected to *both* inter-satellite channels and other down- and up-link channels in the same satellite and thereby used interchangeably for local or inter-satellite service as demand dictates.

System applications and implications

Some potential applications of future technological developments and opportunities have been alluded to in earlier sections, and some implications for policy and institutions may have become apparent. The following treatment of specific services on a case-by-case basis is intended to bring these factors into still sharper focus.

Voice/record services: For several reasons, in domestic and regional communication services of the conventional voice/record type, satellite systems will become very attractive vis-à-vis any terrestrial alternative, particularly where terrestrial network development is rudimentary. The ability to focus full satellite energy on increasingly small areas will reduce the basic cost of satellite circuits to a small fraction of Intelsat's present costs. In addition, the elimination of intermediate switching requirements through use of demand-assigned satellite channels will reduce the total system costs considerably below those for complete terrestrial transmission and switching systems. In areas of extensive terrestrial network development, the marginal add-on cost to established transmission links and switching centers may indeed beat the costs of all-new satellite facilities. But in a comparison of all-new facilities for a total communications capability, satellite systems should prove the most economic, in areas of modest traffic volume, for virtually all long-haul needs including routes of fifty miles or less in length.

In addition to providing low-cost domestic and regional services, these same satellites and associated earth stations can be used for many international services through inter-satellite relays as previously noted. Nations within a single continent or adjacent continents especially, should find this mode of international communication most attractive.

Contrary to some expectations, larger satellites providing both transoceanic and domestic or regional services show little promise of becoming economically desirable. Even with significant economies of scale in the fabrication and launch of such satellites—which seem unlikely based on recent Intelsat experience—other factors militate against this pattern of development. First, it is unlikely that a single satellite could provide both the channel capacity and the reduction in earth station costs needed to make such services viable; both bandwidth and power limitations will have been reached long before the optimum cost trade-off between satellite and earth station is achieved for multi-station systems. Even if this were not the case, satellites located to serve transoceanic routes are inappropriately situated for serving continental routes. None of the Atlantic or Pacific Intelsat satellites is within view of all of the United States or Canada; these satellites are ill-suited to serve the domestic needs of these countries, and the same is true in other areas. Finally, the impossibility of partially repairing a satellite, and the high cost and long lead time of replacing one completely, argue against consolidating such a large amount of critical communications capability in a single facility, even if it were technically and operationally feasible. These considerations are more likely to result in the deployment of many "small" satellites for domestic and regional services, even within a relatively small area, than in the few high-

36

capacity, multi-purpose satellites envisaged by some.

If these projections are anywhere near the mark, they carry major implications for policy and institutions. Should the potential number and capacity of domestic and regional satellite systems greatly exceed that of international systems, the continued domination of planning and development by an international consortium with global participation in design, financing and operation may be difficult to justify. Should inter-satellite relay between domestic and regional systems prove more economic to provide many international communication services, it could erode much of the traffic base on which future growth of the Intelsat system depends.

On the other hand, if promising opportunities for domestic and regional services, including inter-satellite relaying, are simply foreclosed as incompatible with some global plan for satellite development or uninteresting to the dominant members of Intelsat, the public in general and the developing nations in particular could be the losers.

An important consideration which could mitigate some of the potential conflict between domestic/regional and international interests is the need for extensive coordination in design and operation of domestic and regional systems if inter-satellite relay is to be used for international services. An international organization such as Intelsat could well become the agency for such coordination, provided a direct confrontation does not develop between the "single global system" concept and those interested in domestic and regional systems.

Radio-television broadcast services: The satellite's ability to "broadcast" one or more broadband signals over a large geographic area for simultaneous reception by suitable receivers is unparalleled by terrestrial facilities. Whether this capability serves "distribution" purposes (to relatively costly receivers from which further dissemination is made via terrestrial broadcasting, cable, etc.) or "broadcast" purposes (direct to augmented or unaugmented home receivers or community receivers), the first uses of domestic and regional satellites are almost certain to emphasize this type of service. The technology for distribution services is already available; that for direct or community service to augmented receivers essentially could be implemented through a routine two-to-five-year development program given sufficient interest. Direct broadcast to unaugmented home receivers could be achieved within a five-year period if it were economically more attractive than other alternatives; there are no known technological limitations, though it would require further development of energy sources, transmitter tubes and large stabilized antenna structures.

Operational needs and economics point to the very early establishment of radio and television distribution service in areas having well-developed local broadcast and cable systems—probably within the next two or three years. During this same period, community-type broadcast services will be initiated on an experimental basis in India and possibly South American via the NASA ATS-F satellite; economic operational systems of this type could be established within the same time frame but will probably be delayed until their effectiveness for cultural and educational purposes is demonstrated.

In developed areas, satellites for radio and television distribution services may well be distinct from those used for normal voice/record traffic. The volume of traffic involved, the existence of highly competitive alternatives for voice/record traffic, differences between problems of coordinating receive-only versus two-way earth stations with established radio relay systems, and the absence of clear economies of scale beyond a certain traffic volume all point to this possibility. In developing areas, however, for several reasons, the same systems will probably provide both distribution or community broadcast services and limited voice/record service, at least initially. In the first place, use of such facilities primarily for cultural and educational purposes rather than commercial broadcasting may dictate a need for answer-back capability; many educators throughout the world consider this essential to the teaching and learning process. Given the availability of low-cost equipment for demand-assignment of satellite channels, single-channel answer-back capability may not add significantly to the cost of community-type receiving stations. And once such a capability is included for educational purposes, its use for other essential communications (emergency calls, business calls, etc.) seems virtually assured. Furthermore, once any type of earth station facility is available where no other communication facilities exist, satellites are likely to become the most economical means of expanding communications capabilities in areas of low traffic demand, inhospitable terrain, limited commercial activity, etc.

Contrary to some widely expressed forecasts and fears, direct satellite broadcast to unaugmented or even modestly augmented home receivers will probably not become a reality within the foreseeable future. While it will be technologically possible within five or ten years at most, both the operational and the cost effectiveness of this capability are

38

open to serious doubt. In developed areas, the nationwide dissemination of mass information is less pressing than increasing the amount of local programming, to which direct broadcast satellites offer but little; and the nationwide programming that these areas may require can probably be provided more economically via distribution satellites coupled to local broadcast or cable facilities. In developing areas, the basic cost of television receivers for each individual home for cultural and educational purposes will so outweigh the satellite costs that community-type or schoolhouse receivers may prove the only practical solution. Finally as a potential disseminator of propaganda to unwilling nations, TV transmission via direct broadcast satellite to unaugmented (hence unregulatable) receivers would be extremely costly and highly susceptible to jamming by the offended nation. Radio broadcasting, in bands where conventional radio receivers could be reached, presents the same problems and the added fact that propagation back through the earth's ionosphere (below the satellite altitude) is unreliable if not impossible at these frequencies.

Implications for radio resource use and management

In most instances, the same technological developments which render satellites more attractive for domestic and regional communication services also substantially reduce the basis for concern over radio resource scarcity. In particular, the use of very directive satellite antennas to reduce circuit costs also permits multiple use of frequency bands from a given orbital location to different served areas, thereby increasing the communications capacity of the frequency spectrum resource and the number of satellites that the geostationary orbital arc may accommodate.

Domestic or regional satellites employing limited-coverage antenna beams also reduce drastically the need for global coordination of spectrum and orbit use. The United States, Canada and Mexico, for example, will have to coordinate their use of allocated frequencies and that portion of the geostationary orbit within view of these nations; and some coordination between North and South America will be desirable, even though directive satellite antennas will permit both these areas to place satellites in the same orbital locations without mutual interference. Extensive coordination between these continents and Europe or Africa should not be necessary, however, as they will not need common orbital space and will run little risk of mutual interference. Thus the effect of advanced satellite technology and use on frequency use will be to make regional coordination a more pressing concern than the global coordination needed with early satellite technology. The fringe regions will require some global overseeing but is should be much less pervasive than has been envisioned.

A related issue is the concept of orbital "slots" and their allocation and use. As indicated, the transition from global-coverage to limited-coverage satellites permits the geostationary orbital arc to accommodate many more satellites and much greater communications capacity than heretofore seemed feasible; in fact, several satellites serving different geographic areas will be able to occupy essentially the same orbital location (with just enough separation to prevent collisions) and use the same frequency bands without mutual interference. Furthermore, the required separation between satellites serving a common area via common frequency bands is not a constant but a highly variable quantity depending on earth station antenna size and sidelobe characteristics, polarization, modulation technique, type and quality of service desired, etc. Thus not only is there no foreseeable scarcity of orbital "slots," there is no such thing as a discrete orbital slot. With modest technical coordination of satellite emplacement, antenna coverage, and basic design features the number of satellites that can be accommodated is almost unlimited. On the other hand, the excessively rigid allocation of arbitrarily defined slots or orbital sectors to particular nations, users or classes of use could have the effect of a self-fulfilling prophecy, producing the illusion of scarcity through the misuse of abundance. While appropriate mechanisms should be found to protect nations from being denied potential use of the spectrum-orbit resource, the allocation of orbital slots seems neither desirable nor effective as a means to this end.

OTHER TECHNOLOGIES

The emphasis given to communication satellite technology in this paper does not imply that other technologies will occupy insignificant roles in future telecommunication operations. On the contrary, in developed nations with high traffic volumes and highly developed terrestrial networks, not only will existing facilities continue to be used and to grow, but more advanced, high-capacity transmission and switching facilities of the single-route, fixed-capacity type will be in great demand. Despite their flexibility and economic advantages for thin-route services, communications satellite systems do not appear competitive in the

40

near term where communications traffic between nearby cities requires, as it often does in such areas, the use of several thousand circuits.

However, foreseeable advances in terrestrial technologies should have no significant impact on the environment of international communications law. These facilities will continue to provide primarily single-route, fixed-capacity links; they will enjoy increasing economies of scale where traffic density between two points warrants the use of higher capacity links. But in international services the traffic volumes and scale economies that can be anticipated are unlikely to offset the advantages of multiple-route satellites and earth stations, except between immediately adjacent nations where bilateral arrangements will continue to be the *modus operandi*. Transoceanic cables will continue to be touted and established on the basis of redundancy, reliability, and extension of service to regions beyond one-hop satellite coverage; however, they will become increasingly less economic than satellite circuits as both technologies progress, particularly when inter-satellite relay comes into use. High-frequency radio links will continue to be used, but the inherent limitations in capacity and reliability of the ionospheric propagation medium will steadily reduce the importance of such links for basic telecommunications services.

The technological environment of international communications law will be heavily dominated in the foreseeable future by communication satellites. If technical and economic considerations prevail, however, future satellite systems, unlike present systems, will be primarily domestic and regional in scope. Satellites will carry the bulk of international traffic, but inter-satellite relay between domestic or regional satellites serving different areas will handle an increasing proportion of such communications. All these developments will combine to reduce the degree of global participation and coordination required in both satellite system design and operation and spectrum-orbit use and management. However, global oversight of the development of international inter-satellite relays and of spectrum-orbit use where regional interests overlap will continue to be desirable.

Spectrum-orbit resources will not become scarce and the concept of discrete orbital slots will give way to that of a flexible, malleable resource capable of better utilization through coordinated planning and adjustment of technical parameters than through rigid allocation of discrete spatial sectors. Thus the need for highly qualified, independent international advice and coordination will increase, whereas the need for international control and regulation should actually diminish.

Chapter 3

UNILATERALISM IN UNITED STATES SATELLITE
COMMUNICATIONS POLICY

by *Abram Chayes*, Cambridge, Massachusetts

I

In the world of satellite communications, generations of policy issues
succeed each other almost as quickly as generations of hardware. The
current negotiations on Definitive Arrangements for the International
Telecommunications Satellite Consortium—soon to be completed one
way or another—mark the end of an era. During this period, the development of international satellite communications took place largely within the framework of a single unifying and cohesive organization, Intelsat. Legal and institutional problems revolved around the structure and
internal dynamics of that organization. For the United States, the principal questions were the relations of the government, or rather the several concerned agencies of government, to Comsat, the private corporation that is the United States chosen instrument in this field, and through
Comsat to the international organization.

Intelsat was an object and also, it has been said, a creature of United
States policy. In many ways it has been a great success. It has launched
a functioning global system for long-distance communication by satellite,
owned and operated by a public, or at least quasi-public, international
consortium. Its membership has grown from a score of states in 1964 to
more than seventy today, accounting for what must be well over 90 per
cent of the international communications traffic. System costs have been
lower than predicted, by a good deal, and a system performance has
been better. Management, by corporate standards, has been at least adequate and arguably better than that.

One might have thought that the current negotiations on definitive
arrangements would have been the occasion for expanding Intelsat's responsibilities and capacities, for a new burst of organizational energy.
Instead, the new agreements seem likely to limit the further growth of
the organization and to restrict its capacity to serve as an organizing
and unifying force in the field.

It is my view that this seemingly paradoxical result can be traced to a failure of vision and purpose in United States policy—a partial failure only, perhaps, but enough of a failure to account for the result. From the beginning, United States policy-makers recognized the international implications—problems and opportunities—of satellite communications activity. It would have taken a considerable act of will to ignore them. This recognition was accompanied, however, by a distinct ambivalence about solving these problems and pursuing these opportunities in a genuinely international context. Consequently, at critical points, United States policy suffered from an excessive unilateralism that has ended by hamstringing the international instrument created by that policy.

There would be little purpose in reviewing this lugubrious history for its own sake or for the record. The indications are, however, that we may be about to repeat the same errors, perhaps in more virulent form, in the new era now opening. If so, it may not be amiss to point a moral by examining a darker side of the recent past than customarily appears in Comsat's annual reports.

II

From the beginning of the space age, communication by satellite was recognized as an early prospect for commercial development. Research and development moved forward in the United States at a pace such that President Kennedy was moved to make a basic policy statement in the summer of 1961,[1] a full year before the first successful Telstar experiment. That first statement was flawed by the duality of purpose that has marked all subsequent United States policy in the field. For although President Kennedy invited "all nations to participate in a communications satellite system, in the interest of world peace and closer brotherhood among peoples throughout the world," he also opted for "private ownership and operation of the U.S. portion of the system." More broadly the statement called for United States leadership in the rapid development of commercial satellite communications.

The preference for private ownership was apparently qualified. It was to be maintained only if compatible with a long list of other objectives specified in the statement, including global coverage, foreign participation in the system through ownership or otherwise, and non-discriminatory use and equitable access to the system. In the event, none of these

[1] "Statement by the President on Communication Satellite Policy," John F. Kennedy, *Public Papers of the Presidents,* I (1961): 529.

specific objectives was found to be frustrated by private ownership of the United States portion of the system. Thus the President's announced preference settled the issue. The choice, whatever its justification in terms of domestic politics or the supposed genius of the American system, meant from the outset that United States foreign policy objectives and perceptions in this field would be filtered through a private entity with divergent goals and perspectives. Under the circumstances, it is not surprising that the State Department, almost alone among the agencies advising the President, recommended that United States satellite development should be pursued through a government owned corporation. It will not be surprising either, to long-time observers of the Department, that its views were pressed with only a modicum of skill or energy.

The legislative battle over the Communications Satellite Act of 1962,[2] was principally about the form private ownership should take, and is thus not really relevant to the present discussion. What is significant for these purposes is the curious failure of Congress to grasp the international ramifications of the enterprise it was setting afoot. To be sure, the legislation makes appropriate genuflection to "world peace and understanding," to "providing services to economically less developed countries" and to "non-discriminatory access to the system." But, although President Kennedy's statement had spoken of "the U.S. *portion* of the system," most Congressmen, I think it fair to say, conceived of the proposed global system as a United States show. It was to be not unlike the Union Pacific, another company chartered by Act of Congress: anyone could ride, but it was our railroad. This conception shows up most clearly in Section 201(c)(3) of the statute, to date unused, authorizing the Federal Communications Commission to require Comsat to establish satellite communications to any particular foreign point upon the advice of the Secretary of State that such action should be taken in the national interest. This authority is a common feature of state and federal statutes regulating public utilities in the United States, but it sounds anomalous, to say the least, as applied to an internationally owned satellite system.

No doubt Congressmen who were better schooled in the telecommunication field could not be quite so oblivious to the international realities involved. Apparently they looked to the financing and operating arrangements that had been used for transoceanic cables as a model. The practice has been for the American carrier, usually American Telephone and Telegraph, to make a separate deal for each of these facilities with its

2 47 U.S.C. §§ 701-44 (1964).

44

counterpart administrations abroad. Ordinarily these have been bilateral joint ventures, with the parties at each end of the line sharing equally in the costs and revenues of the cable operation. Occasionally, several European administrations have arranged to get channels in the cable by sharing in ownership at the European end; and likewise, after the Federal Communications Commission began to show solicitude for the future of smaller American carriers, there was some multiple participation in the United States half of each venture.

This form of organization has two salient features. First, the owners of the cable at either terminus stand astride the lines of communication. Users further along the route—for instance the interior countries of Europe—do not have direct access to the cable. They must pay the owning administration to relay their messages. Second, the resulting pattern is a web of separate cables with its center in the United States, and more particularly with the major United States carrier, A.T. & T.

Certainly this was the original conception of the officers of Comsat. They talked of the satellite as a "cable in the sky." And their first effort at international negotiations was a round of visits to the chief European administrations, in London, Paris and Bonn, to explore the possibilities of a joint venture agreement patterned essentially on the cable arrangements. As an alternative they offered the prospect of leasing channels in an American owned and operated satellite.

At this remove, one wonders how serious hopes for success could have been entertained for these proposals. As we know, they were countered by the formation of the European Conference on Satellite Communications, an affiliate of CEPT, which developed a unified position insisting on some form of multilateral negotiation and organization for the intercontinental satellite system. Cooler and wiser heads in Canada and to some extent Japan reinforced this position.

The United States State Department was a shorn Samson. A combination of practical appraisal of the international political situation and idealistic yearning for an international institution led it to support the kind of multinational effort the Europeans seemed to want. But the Department had to operate in terms of a statute and Congressional background that seemed to contemplate United States hegemony, at the least, in the global system. Moreover, the Department's ability to influence events in any other direction was seriously if not fatally impaired by the fact that in the United States internal policy discussions it had favored public ownership of the United States satellite company.

As a result, the State Department, and thus to some extent the United

States government as a whole, was confined to an indirect influence on the course of the negotiations. The Department's approach was therefore to contrive repeatedly to expose the officers of the company to situations, meetings and conferences where they could experience, as uncomfortably as could be arranged, the international realities of the situation. Gradually this process took its toll, and Comsat was brought to the realization that some form of international mechanism for ownership of the international system was essential. It also brought the United States government, in return, to support Comsat's demands for dominating authority in the international consortium.

The Interim Arrangements provided for this authority by giving Comsat decisive voting power and making it the manager for the Intelsat consortium. The voting arrangements gave Comsat an undisplaceable majority and thus a veto over any action of the consortium. Moreover the provisions are such that the concurrence of only two or three of the other major countries is needed to enforce Comsat's affirmative views. The managership is, also, a source of independent power perhaps beyond what the title by itself conveys. For under the terms of the Interim Arrangements, the manager initiates action on all important matters. It prepares the budget, proposes contractors, negotiates and recommends contracts, and the like.[3] Comsat, as an English observer remarked in rueful retrospect, "was not only Lord High Executioner, but Lord High Everything Else."

The result was a hybrid. The forms of international action, and indeed a good bit of the substance, were accepted. An international agency like Intelsat takes on a life of its own and tends to impose its own constraints regardless of the formal distribution of powers. But the Interim Arrangements did not provide the conditions for the growth of confidence in the consortium as an international instrument responsive to the international community. Intelsat became, for the most part, an arena in which Americans and Europeans battled out and traded out parochial interests without achieving a larger vision of international communications requirements.

Comsat's dominance in Intelsat was not bought without a price. The price was a limit of five years on the duration of the Interim Arrangements. At the time, Comsat's officers said that if they could not prove themselves in that time they would deserve to be displaced. One could pursue the details of the ways, some of them wondrous, in which over

[3] See Art. 9, 12, Special Agreement, Aug. 20, 1964, [1964] 2 U.S.T. 1745, T.I.A.S. No. 5646, 514 U.N.T.S. 48.

46

the ensuing five years Comsat tried to prove itself worthy. But it is doubtful that Comsat could have followed any program that could have brought it a vote of confidence at the end of the five years. The seeds of distrust and resistance had already been sown.

The dénouement, some would say the predictable dénouement, has come at the year-long Plenipotentiary Conference on Definitive Arrangements, now, one hopes, in its final phases. And the result that appears likely at this writing is, in a sense, the worst of both worlds. Comsat's position will be significantly impaired. Of course, the United States representative to the organization will always speak with a powerful voice. The technical and financial contribution of the United States ensures that. But Comsat's formal powers will be drastically reduced. Its vote will be in the neighborhood of 40 per cent and its veto will be eliminated. More important, its term as manager will end five years hence.

On the other hand, even with the position of the United States thus reduced, the other members have been unwilling to vest Intelsat with broad and comprehensive responsibility for international satellite communications. At the present writing, the organization is not prohibited from providing regional and specialized forms of satellite communications services. But because it can enter new fields only with the consent of the Assembly, bold planning for a comprehensive and integrated system will not be possible.

The result will be, in my view, that Intelsat will settle into the accepted and conventional role of an intercontinental carrier of commercial voice and message traffic. That will be a welcome and useful addition to the world's international communications faciliters, and one should not disparage that accomplishment. But the future development of satellite communications will occur outside the framework of the consortium.

III

I said at the outset that my purpose in reviewing this recent history was not simply to bury the past or to exhume it. In the new period with its new problems that is now beginning there is already evidence in United States policy of the same excessive unilateralism that marked it in the past.

If I am right that Intelsat cannot be counted on as a comprehensive, integrating agency for satellite communications, the period ahead will see the proliferation of a number of geographically or functionally specialized systems. Coordination among these systems, particularly as regards use of the frequency spectrum and the orbital arc, will be of the first importance. There is every reason to think that these resources, wisely used, will provide ample communications capacity for all. But wise use depends on advance international planning and harmonization of projected systems. Without some such activity, we are likely to see ill-advised pre-emptive actions of various kinds, taken in the hope of preserving future freedom of action but having the result of reducing total spectrum availability, perhaps to such an extent that a real shortage could ensue.

As was the case a decade ago, the United States has made the first move in the new policy setting for satellite communications. A White House Memorandum issued on January 23, 1970 outlines policy recommendations for United States domestic satellite systems.[4] At least on the surface the Memorandum is reminiscent of earlier policy pronouncements—President Kennedy's statement and the Communications Satellite Act of 1962—in its balancing of national and international considerations. There is the same reference to the international dimensions: "the international aspects of geostationary orbital and radio resources," "obligations and commitments to Intelsat and the International Telecommunications Union" and "other foreign policy considerations." Yet the main thrust of the Memorandum is to urge the FCC to authorize the establishment of United States domestic systems as a matter of national decision in the portion of the orbital arc that the United States necessarily shares with Canada and Latin America.

Let me make it perfectly clear that I am *not* saying that the White House recommendations disregarded the interests of those other countries. On the contrary, there is every indication that they were taken fully into account. The Memorandum says:

> Since some of the orbital locations and associated spectrum usage of interest for United States domestic satellites might also be potentially useful to other western hemisphere nations, a question of United States monopolization could conceivably arise. However, even 10 to 12 United States domestic satellites (a high estimate of likely early system development) would represent only a small fraction of the number which could be accommodated for western hemisphere use with the current state of the art. Therefore, orbital capacity is not expected to be a problem at this time.

I am prepared to agree with that conclusion. After all it is my White

[4] Memorandum for the Hon. Dean Burch, Chairman, Federal Communications Commission, White House press release, Jan. 23, 1970.

House. But why should Canada or Latin America accept a United States determination—unsupported, it must be said, by technical analysis or documentation—that there will be plenty left over after we take all we want for ourselves. That has not been the experience with any other potentially scarce resource. Moreover, so far as I can determine, there was no effort to consult with affected countries before the United States decision was reached and the Memorandum issued. Even if the United States has acted responsibly on the merits, as I am convinced it has, that is not the kind of behavior in this field it should be prepared to encourage by example.

There is ground for further concern in the White House Memorandum. It states that "As demand for satellite communication expands, it may become necessary to evolve additional coordinating mechanisms." This acknowledgement is grudging enough, but the Memorandum goes on to say that the need, if it arises, should be met by establishing "appropriate technical standards rather than rationing orbital positions." One can agree that a rationing approach should be avoided. But the alternative is not necessarily to elaborate technical standards, presumably of general application and made, amended and carried out by existing ITU machinery. This kind of system although only briefly adumbrated in the Memorandum, seems calculated to carry forward the first-come-first-served bias of existing ITU procedure, to the primary benefit of the United States and two or three other countries with present access to the medium. Moreover, it seems too rigid and difficult to adapt to the rapidly changing needs and capabilities of a new technology. If so, the system would neither deserve nor be likely to attract widespread international support.

IV

In my view the United States should begin to face up fully to the international implications of its satellite communication policy. At a minimum this requires a recognition that the frequency spectrum and orbital arc are international resources subject to international management and decision making processes. As a practical consequence of this recognition, the United States should begin now, even before adequate international machinery is established, to consult in detail with its neighbors in this hemisphere about its domestic satellite communications policy. The FCC should not authorize and the National Aeronautics and Space Adminis-

49

tration should not launch any domestic communications satellite without full advance consultation with all affected countries.

For the longer term, the United States should support the creation of adequate international machinery for spectrum management, probably within the framework of ITU. The requirement, it is true, is not for allocation of orbital space or harsh regulation of spectrum use. On the contrary it is for a mechanism supple enought to take advantage of design possibilities and an advancing technology so as to accommodate all of the many demands that are likely to be made on these resources. Above all the institution must be able to command confidence that its judgments are truly independant and do not represent, in masked form, the policy interests of any one country. If ITU is to assume such responsibility, as seems logical, ITU itself must be significantly strengthened and this should be a central object of United States policy.

The time has come for the United States to stop trying to have it both ways—to acknowledge the essentially international interests in satellite communications and at the same time to preserve substantially unfettered national freedom of action. The United States will necessarily have a large, an all-but-decisive role in any system of satellite communications, given its launch capabilities, its mastery of the technology and its share of the traffic. But it should make up its mind to use that influence subject to the constraints of genuinely international decision-making institutions. In the end, maximum freedom of action for the United States and for other nations as well will derive not from unilateral action, no matter how well intended, but from orderly cooperative development of what is after all an international medium. The United States should bend its example and its efforts to ensuring that development.

Chapter 4

INTERNATIONAL INSTITUTIONS FOR TELE-COMMUNICATIONS: THE ITU'S ROLE

by *Harold Karan Jacobson,* Ann Arbor, Michigan

I

The International Telecommunication Union (ITU) is the oldest of the agencies of the United Nations family, tracing its origins to the International Telegraph Convention signed in Paris in 1865. Since then, despite crises and even wars among its members, ITU has been in continuous existence. Its present mandate, institutions and mode of operations are the product of this long history.

That ITU is the most venerable of the U.N. agencies should not be surprising. In few fields is the need for international collaboration so obvious as it is in communications. Since about 1800, technological developments—first the telegraph, then the telephone, and then radio and television—have enormously enhanced man's ability to transmit increasingly complex messages rapidly over long distances, and at substantially decreasing costs. Today, oral and visual messages transmitted through communications satellites can circle the globe in just a few seconds. But the globe is divided into sovereign states, and they must cooperate if they are to reap the full benefits of this technological progress.

States could, of course, confine their communications within their own boundaries, but for several reasons they choose not to do so. Commerce is a major one. A nation that engages in trade and seeks to enjoy the benefits of specialization requires an ability to communicate across state borders. States also have political relations with one another which can be facilitated by communications: even adversaries can find it helpful to communicate. When communications must cross borders, however, only international collaboration can assure that they will reach their destinations.

Even the simple telegraph required substantial cooperation. Messages could be physically carried across borders, and they were. A much more efficient system, however, was to connect the telegraph lines of adjacent states. The establishment of such a system required at least a measure of agreement on the standardization of equipment, operating procedures and, to a lesser extent, administrative procedures, including rates for services. More complex technology required correspondingly more elaborate agreements. The development of radio communication utilizing the frequency spectrum added a new dimension to the requirement for collaboration among states, the careful selection of frequencies, without which radio transmitters can cause harmful interference to one another.

The obvious benefits to be gained from international collaboration have generally been compelling, and starting with the 1849 treaty between Austria and Prussia providing for the linking of their telegraph lines, international cooperative arrangements have closely followed technological developments. It soon became apparent that multilateral, and indeed potentially universal or quasi-universal, agreements would in most instances bring greater benefits than bilateral agreements; the first multilateral instruments were signed only a few years after the Austrian-Prussian treaty. The 1865 Conference in Paris, though, was a milestone, for it not only was attended by representatives of twenty states including all of those that were then considered important in world politics, but also established an institutional frame-work to facilitate collaborative efforts, the International Telegraph Union.

Three years later, in 1868, the members of the Union took another far-reaching step, the establishment of a permanent bureau, and gradually the Union expanded its functions. In 1885 it began to draft regulations for the telephone. It assumed further responsibilities when the International Radio Telegraph Union, which had been created in 1906, was merged with it at the Madrid Conference in 1932. At this Conference the present name, the International Telecommunication Union, was chosen, a modification which allowed the acronym ITU to remain unchanged.

While ITU is testimony to the virtual necessity for collaboration among states, it and its history also reflect the desire of states to retain maximum control over communication processes. Communication systems could have been organized on an international basis and ITU or some similar body given responsibility for their operation. Instead, communication systems have generally been organized within individual nations with operational responsibility assigned to national entities. Occasionally groups of nations have joined together to organize and operate communication systems. Intelsat (the International Telecommunications Satellite Consortium) is the most comprehensive of these, but even it does not have universal membership. States have insisted on maintaining control of communication systems individually or sharing control

52

only with friendly states, primarily because of the importance of such systems to the civilian and military functions of government. Governments feel that their ability to control their citizens and to pursue their chosen policies might be seriously jeopardized if they did not have control of their communication systems.

The functions which states are willing to assign to ITU therefore have been limited to facilitating connections among systems and to preventing these systems from interfering with one another. States have seen ITU as a framework within which they could settle such matters by bargaining among themselves, not as an independant, decision-making agency. They have viewed the Secretariat mainly as a body that services conferences and have never been enthusiastic about building up either its powers or its staff. This has been true from the outset. The only controversial issue at the Paris Conference in 1865 was whether or not a permanent bureau was needed, and three years elapsed before the negative decision taken then was reversed.

Viewed in one perspective, the unwillingness of states to assign more than the most limited functions to ITU might be regarded as a serious liability for the organization. It has certainly served to constrain the Union's growth. In another perspective, though, it may actually have been an asset, for had the Union had more extensive functions, particularly in the operation of communication systems, it might not have been able to weather the many crises among its members that it has successfully withstood. ITU's limited role has served to insulate it from the ebb and flow of tensions in world politics.

Despite these limitations, ITU's functions have involved the provision of a kind of technical assistance to its less developed members. For example, its recommendations concerning specifications for equipment have provided useful guidelines for such states. And as less developed states have increased, substantially in ITU's membership, its technical assistance activities have expanded. In 1950 the Union decided to participate in the United Nations Expanded Program of Technical Assistance, and since then providing technical assistance to developing countries has become an increasingly important ITU activity. The financing for this activity, however, has not come from the ITU but from the United Nations itself, partly because the degree of commitment among ITU members has traditionally been limited. Technical assistance can be classified merely as another way of facilitating collaboration among communication systems, since it involves creating systems with which those already in existence can collaborate.

The International Telecommunication Union's present mandate, as defined in the Convention negotiated at the Montreux Conference in 1965, is broadly "to maintain and extend international cooperation for the improvement and rational use of telecommunications of all kinds."[1] ITU is also charged with promoting "the development of technical facilities and their most efficient operation." More specifically, ITU's functions are to:

(a) effect allocation of the radio frequency spectrum and registration of radio frequency assignments;

(b) coordinate efforts to eliminate harmful interference between radio stations of different countries and to improve the use made of the radio frequency spectrum;

(c) foster collaboration with respect to the establishment of the lowest possible rates;

(d) foster the creation, development and improvement of telecommunication equipment and networks in new or developing countries by every means at its disposal, especially its participation in the appropriate programs of the United Nations;

(e) promote the adoption of measures for ensuring the safety of life through the cooperation of telecommunication services;

(f) undertake studies, make regulations, adopt resolutions, formulate recommendations and opinions, and collect and publish information concerning telecommunications matters for the benefit of all Members and Associate Members.

Of these specific functions, (b) and (d) were added when the Telecommunication Convention was revised in 1959 at the Geneva Conference; the others have been unchanged since the major revision of the Convention in 1947 at the Atlantic City Conference. All of them are fairly narrowly defined.

II

To perform these functions the members of ITU have created a complex institutional structure. As determined by the Montreux Plenipotentiary Conference in 1965, ITU consists of: the Plenipotentiary Conference; Administrative Conferences; the Administrative Council; and the so-called permanent organs, including (a) the General Secretariat, (b) the International Frequency Registration Board (IFRB), (c) the International Radio Consultative Committee (CCIR) and (d) the International Telegraph and Telephone Consultative Committee (CCITT).

The Plenipotentiary Conference is the supreme organ of the Interna-

[1] International Telecommunication Convention (Montreux, 1965), Art. 4.

tional Telecommunication Union. It consists of delegations of all members and associate members. It meets irregularly, roughly every five years. Its most important functions are to determine ITU's general policies, establish the basis for the budget and determine a fiscal limit for expenditures, and revise the Telecommunication Convention if it considers such revision necessary. In addition, it elects the Secretary-General, the Deputy Secretary-General and the members of ITU who serve on the Administrative Council.

The Administrative Council consists of twenty-nine members who meet annually and could meet more often. It oversees the administration of the Union and in certain instances acts on behalf of the Plenipotentiary Conference.

Administrative Conferences, either global, or regional, are normally convened to consider specific telecommunication matters. Their principal function is the periodic partial or complete revision of the Telegraph Regulations, the Telephone Regulations, the Radio Regulations and the Additional Radio Regulations, which are collectively called the Administrative Regulations. In addition, World Administrative Conferences dealing with radio communication elect the five members of the International Frequency Registration Board. Although only member states have privileges in the Administrative Conferences, non-members, including representative of recognized private operating agencies also attend the sessions.

The International Consultative Committees study and issue recommendations concerning technical and operating questions. The CCIR and CCITT operate through *ad hoc* working parties, Study Groups, World and Regional Plan Committees, and Plenary Assemblies. Plenary Assemblies meet every three years. Only they can adopt formal recommendations; they also elect the Directors of the CCIR and CCITT. Recognized private operating agencies and scientific and industrial organizations as well as members and associate members of ITU may participate in the work of the International Consultative Committees. Only ITU member states may vote in the Plenary Assemblies, but if a state is absent, the recognized private operating agencies of that country may, acting as a whole, cast a single vote.

The secretariat of the International Telecommunication Union consists of four quite distinct parts, each of which is headed by one or more elected officials. The largest is the General Secretariat, with a staff of more than 250, directed by the Secretary-General and the Deputy Secretary-General. The International Frequency Registration Board is the second largest component. Headed by its five elected members, the IFRB has a staff of about one hundred. Finally, the CCIR and the CCITT each have a staff of about twenty-five or thirty headed by an elected Director. In all, ITU has nine elected officials and an appointed staff of over four hundred. The elected heads of each component of the secretariat are chosen by and work with slightly different constituencies, which could impel them toward somewhat different orientations.

In a sense emphasizing the independence of these components, the Montreux Convention provided for a Coordination Committee consisting of the Secretary-General, the Deputy Secretary-General, the Directors of the International Consultative Committees and the Chairman of the International Frequency Registration Board. The Convention admonished this Committee to reach conclusions unanimously and allows the Secretary-General to act without the support of two or more of its members only in matters that he judges to be urgent. When the matter is not urgent, the Convention provides that it should be referred to the Administrative Council.

To a substantial extent the complexity of the institutional structure of ITU is a result of its long history and evolution. When new functions have been added to the Union, they have usually resulted in new organs being grafted onto the previously existing structure. Such organs have gained a certain legitimacy, making it difficult to consider abolishing, amalgamating or even revising them. The complexity is also a result of the unwillingness of states to grant substantial powers to the Union. Having many elected officials and requiring that disagreements among them be referred to the Administrative Council is a way of limiting the autonomy of the secretariat. Finally, the complexity is also a result of the technical nature of ITU's province. It is designed to facilitate the participation of specialists in the consideration of technical questions, and it recognizes that specialists are not equally adept in all aspects of ITU's activities. Many of ITU's organs are consequently structured around particular substantive and technical problems.

III

With this understanding of ITU's historical development, mandate and institutional structure, it is now possible to consider its mode of operation, how it performs its functions. It is appropriate to concentrate first on ITU's traditional functions of facilitating connections among systems and making arrangements to ensure that these systems do not interfere with one another. The treatment here will be evaluative as well as descriptive.

Facilitating connections among communication systems requires a measure of standardization of operating and administrative procedures as well as of equipment. The activities of the International Consultative Committees contribute to these objectives. These Committees adopt a vast number of recommendations covering a wide range of topics. For example, at the Plenary Assembly of the CCITT in Mar del Plata, Argentina, in 1968, recommendations were adopted on the issuance of credit cards to telecommunication users, a new international telegraph alphabet, specifications for echo suppressors and a host of other subjects. The recommendations adopted at the Plenary Assembly of an International Consultative Committee fill several volumes.

Study Groups take the initial steps in framing recommendations which, however, can only be formally adopted by Plenary Assemblies and technically by majority vote there. The recommendations are merely that; they have no binding power. Nevertheless, there is considerable pressure to comply with them, for only thus can connections among systems be made.

Frequently the recommendations have substantial financial implications. Local communications systems are usually designed with local conditions in mind, and consequently there are many variations among them. Connecting them can require modifications in one or more of the systems. In cases of this nature, the recommendations of the International Consultative Committees will determine how the burdens of making modifications will be distributed. When new technology is involved, recommendations specifying standards may mean giving legitimacy to certain patent holders and not to others. Recommendations can obviously involve millions of dollars.

Both because of the non-binding character of recommendations and the substantial financial stakes involved, great efforts are made in the International Consultative Committees to achieve consensus and unanimity. Although majority voting is the formal rule in Plenary Assemblies, it is almost never invoked. Plenary Assemblies generally accept the conclusions of Study Groups with little or no modification. Although all members of the International Consultative Committees can participate in the Study Groups, usually only a few do. The participants in the Study Groups generally come from the states most advanced technically in the field of telecommunications—the United States, the Soviet Union, Japan, the United Kingdom, France, the Federal Republic of Germany, Canada, Czechoslovakia, Italy, Belgium and the Netherlands. The Study Groups proceed on the basis of technical papers. The participants have to be technically competent, and they are generally sophisticated about their colleagues' positions, problems and power. Recommendations are framed through a process of mutual adjustment in which economic and technical costs are carefully weighed and apportioned. Influence varies with the issue being considered, but it is almost never distributed equally. For instance, it would be extremely unlikely that a recommendation concerning telephones would be formulated which did not take into careful account the interests of the United States, which has almost half the telephones in service in the world. Since the objective of participating in the activities of the International Consultative Committees is to make it possible to communicate with others, the unequal distribution of influence in Study Groups seldom results in states' exercising veto powers. Rather it means that all participants will compromise, but some will compromise more than others.

The outstanding achievement of the International Consultative Committees is the formulation of a tremendous number of recommendations that are generally followed. Compliance is very high. There are only two notable instances in which it has been impossible to agree on recommendations, both involving the CCIR. Despite considerable effort, the CCIR could not formulate recommendations concerning specifications for equipment for black-and-white and color television. As a consequence different television systems are now employed in different parts of the world, and the reception of programs transmitted from stations of one system by receivers designed for another is difficult. Other than these two instances, however, the ability of the CCI's to achieve agreement has been exceptionally good.

Acknowledging this substantial achievement, two criticisms have been leveled against the International Consultative Committees by ITU members and informed observers. The first is that the process of formulating recommendations is too time-consuming, especially in view of the rapid pace of technological advance in the field of telecommunications. The process of mutual adjustment in Study Groups is slow, and recommendations must be adopted at Plenary Assemblies, which meet only every three years. Several years may elapse from the introduction of an issue to the adoption of a recommendation. Critics argue that this time lag holds back technological progress. It can, they maintain, restrain the production of equipment or result in the production of incompatible

58

equipment. Defenders of the present system point out that almost all issues are technically complex and that the process of the mutual adjustment of interests is necessarily time-consuming. They also assert that once a Study Group has reached a conclusion, it is possible to assume that this will become a recommendation without waiting for its formal adoption by a Plenary Assembly. Nevertheless, there seems to be growing sentiment within ITU for the adoption of some procedure that would make possible more rapid action where it was generally felt to be necessary.

The second criticism of the International Consultative Committees is that they pay insufficient attention to the problems and interests of ITU's less developed member states. This criticism is two-pronged. First, the charge is made that the subjects considered are disproportionately those that concern primarily the developed states. Secondly, it is alleged that the recommendations pay insufficient attention to the interests of the developing countries. To amplify this point, since the recommendations frequently involve systems with several variables, many trade-offs are possible, for instance between cost and versatility. The interests of states in these trade-offs will vary, depending among other things on their level of economic development.

Whether or not this criticism has merit is difficult to judge. In certain instances the most advanced technology may be more economical for less developed than for highly developed states, given the heavy investment of the latter in existing equipment. In any case, it is not difficult to understand why the processes of the International Consultative Committees could leave ITU's less developed members uneasy. Inputs come almost exclusively from highly developed states, and bargains are struck among their representatives. Given the small size of the staffs of the two CCI's, they can hardly do more than provide the necessary administrative services for meetings.

Few changes are realistically possible in this area. The work of the International Consultative Committees depends on a high level of technical expertise. The repositories of such expertise are the manufacturers of telecommunication equipment and the operators of telecommunication systems, which are located mainly in the developed countries of the world. Nor are the facts that almost half of the telephones in service in the world are located in the United States and that communications occur predominantly among the developed states of the Atlantic area, Oceania and Japan likely to change quickly. Still, if the CCI's staffs had more extensive technical resources, they might be in a position to provide more substantial inputs to the work of the committees, inputs which could be less colored by the interest of the developed states.

Issues requiring the elaboration of standards which are of a more fundamental and permanent nature than those treated by the recommendations of the International Consultative Committees are dealt with by ITU through the Administrative Regulations, which are revised by Administrative Conferences. The present Administrative Regulations are products of long evolution, some provisions dating from the Union's earliest days. The Telegraph Regulations and the Telephone Regulations were revised most recently in 1958, and the Radio Regulations and Additional Radio Regulations in 1959, with further partial revisions in 1963 (dealing with space), in 1966 (dealing with aeronautical services) and in 1967 (dealing with maritime services).

The Administrative Regulations are adopted by a majority of those present and voting in Administrative Conferences. Article 15 of the Telecommunication Convention states that ratification of the Convention involves "acceptance" of the Administrative Regulations in force at the time of ratification or accession. The same article obliges members to inform the Secretary-General of ITU of their approval of any revision of these Regulations. Presumably the Regulations are binding on those states which have approved them, but generally there is no mechanism for enforcement other than the permission granted to states not to apply certain provisions, particularly those relating to rates in the case of states which themselves do not apply these provisions. In other words, retaliation is permissible. However, the vast majority of ITU members approve the periodic revisions of the Administrative Regulations, and even those that do not tend to apply most of their provisions. Again, the desire to communicate provides a powerful pressure toward compliance.

To this point attention has been focused on those aspects of ITU's traditional functions relating to facilitating connections among systems. Another traditional function, which is partially discharged through the Administrative Regulations, is that of making arrangements to ensure that communication systems do not interfere with one another. This pertains to all systems which rely completely or partly on the transmission through air of electric waves-radio and television, obviously, but also some telegraph and telephone systems. Stations transmitting on the same radio frequency could under certain circumstances interfere with one another and make reception of their signals difficult or impossible. States have given ITU several functions intended to prevent such interference.

60

First, ITU is charged with the allocation of the radio frequency spectrum. This is done in Administrative Conferences. There, certain frequency bands are allocated for specific purposes, for example maritime mobile, broadcasting, aeronautical radio navigation, land mobile, amateur and space. Some allocations are made on a global basis, others vary among three regions. Roughly, Region I consists of Western Europe, Africa, the USSR and Mongolia; Region II, the Americas; and Region III, the remainder of Asia and Oceania. Additional distinctions are made for the tropical zone, a band which varies slightly with the three regions but which roughly includes the area between the parallels 30 degrees north and 35 degrees south. The allocations agreed to in the Administrative Conference are embodied in the Radio Regulations.

Assignment to stations or users of specific frequencies within these allocations is the responsibility of member states. In the United States, for instance, the Federal Communications Commission performs this function. The Radio Regulations require that all assignments which are to be used for international radio communication, which might cause harmful interference with services of other states or for which international recognition is desired should be reported to the International Frequency Registration Board. The Board then notifies all member states of this assignment and checks to see if it conforms with the Telecommunication Convention and the Table of Frequency Allocations or is likely to cause harmful interference with a frequency assignment already recorded in its Master Register. If the Board's findings are favorable, the assignment will be recorded in the Master Register as of the date of receipt. The Board receives an average of more than 1,700 assignments each week and gives favorable findings in at least 70 per cent of the cases.

Should the Board find that the assignment is likely to cause harmful interference, it will return the notice to the authority which made the assignment with its findings and perhaps suggestions for a solution. If a state insists on maintaining a frequency assignment despite an unfavorable finding by the Board, it may nonetheless gain recognition for the assignment, for the Regulations provide that if an assignment has been in use for at least sixty days without the Board's receiving a complaint of harmful interference the assignment shall be recorded in the Master Register.

If assignments are notified before being brought into use and then not brought into use within 120 days, the Board may cancel the entry in the Master Register. The Board may also cancel or alter entries if

61

the use of an assignment has been discontinued or if the use does not accord with the basic characteristics specified in the notification, but only with the agreement of the notifying administration.

Once an assignment is entered in the Master Register, it has international recognition. In practical terms, this means that the assignment has a certain legitimacy. This is significant, for it is generally in all parties' interest to avoid harmful interference; and thus there a strong pressure against ignoring entries on the Master Register. However, if a party is determined to do so, ITU has no powers to impose sanctions. States can report cases of harmful interference to the International Frequency Registration Board, but the most that the Board can do is to study the problem and suggest possible ways of solving it. The Radio Regulations leave the solution of the problem to the conflicting parties, merely admonishing them to act in good faith.

While the IFRB's powers have never been more extensive than they now are, when the Board was first created at the Atlantic City Conference in 1947 a number of Americans who were principally responsible for its creation hoped that it would enter, even with its modest powers, into the field of frequency management. They saw it as something of a cross between the Federal Communications Commission and the International Court of Justice. Several states, and particularly the Soviet Union, never agreed with this conception, and in its actual operations the Board has fallen far short of it. According to the 1947 revision of the Telecommunication Convention, the Board could take the initiative in furnishing advice to members "with a view to the operation of the maximum practicable number of radio channels in those positions of the spectrum where harmful interference may occur."[2] For a variety of reasons the Board has not developed this role extensively, though the provision has remained in the Convention. Nor has it developed extensively a mediatory role in cases of harmful interference. Instead, the Board has become a rather passive body, primarily responding to notifications of assignments. At the Montreux Conference in 1965 the United States argued that the Board could be abolished, that its functions could be performed by the Secretariat. This was in sharp contrast to the United States position at the Geneva Conference in 1959, when it argued that the members of the Board should be appointed for life to ensure their impartiality. On neither occasion was the United States position adopted.

How adequate ITU's system of frequency allocation and registration

[2] International Telecommunication Convention (Atlantic City, 1947), Art. 6.

62

is in terms of modern communication needs is a matter of controversy. Many maintain that the system is as good as could reasonably be expected, given the basic desire of states to retain control over their communication facilities. Others are critical. The system of effecting allocations through Administrative Conferences has been attacked by representatives of both developed and less developed states. Some of the former are uneasy about having such a complicated technical matter decided by majority vote in a forum where the technical qualifications of the participants are not assured. They have an ingrained distrust of voting as a way of settling such matters, and they are disdainful of the technical competence of some participants. Some representatives of less developed countries, on the other hand, feel overpowered by the developed countries with their immense technical resources. For instance, the United States spent two years preparing for the 1963 Extraordinary Administrative Radio Conference convened to consider problems of telecommunications in space. Beyond those in the government who worked on the preparation of the United States position, major studies were undertaken by several private corporations. No other country was as well prepared and none could have been.

If pressed, however, neither side in this controversy can point to substantial specific needs which have been ignored in the frequency allocation process. Furthermore, it is hard to conceive of a fundamentally different system that would be widely accepted. There is little evidence that states would be willing to turn such a sensitive matter over to a group of experts or a small council of governmental representatives. Perhaps to put it more accurately, they might agree to assign this function to a small group, but then the composition of this group would become crucial, and the possibility of reaching agreement on this would be extremely remote. The present system does give each state a voice, and some, because of their greater technical resources, gain greater influence.

Both groups, however, have raised less sweeping issues. Some economists and engineers from developed states have argued that the present system of effecting allocations is too rigid and consequently inefficient, wasteful and ill-adapted to a field where technological progress is extremely rapid. They allege that once an allocation has been made it will seldom be changed, and they maintain that since many services are quite local the allocations need not cover areas as large as the three regions, much less the globe. In their view the present system results in certain portions of the spectrum being subjected to great pressure while other portions are underutilized. They would like to see greater flexibility. One argument against this stems from the heavy capital investment often required to develop a radio communication system. Individuals might be reluctant to undertake such investment if they felt that within a short time they would have to make alterations to take account of new allocations. Still, some midpoint might be found which would allow greater flexibility and room for experimentation than the present system and still not inhibit investment or, worse yet, invite chaos.

Some governmental officials from developing states fear that the present system is mainly responsible to those states which have the technical resources to foresee and express their needs—that is, the developed states. These officials worry that their needs, which they have difficulty foreseeing, will be slighted. In this view the radio frequency spectrum is a limited resource, and allocation to one purpose precludes others. Similar fears have also been expressed by user groups such as radio astronomers, who are ordinarily not well represented in state delegations to ITU conferences. One way of easing these fears somewhat might be to build up the technical competence of ITU's staff and allow it, and perhaps even require it, to make a greater substantive contribution in ITU conferences. Being responsible only to the Union, it would be relatively disinterested and in a position to present broad public interest concerns. ITU staff work could serve to supplement the technical resources of the less developed countries. Decisions, of course, would continue to be made by states. The purpose of the change would be to work toward making all relevant information available before decisions are made and to strengthen the position of some of the weaker participants. Greater flexibility in the allocations might also help to meet some of these fears. As this implies, with proper management multiple uses of the frequency spectrum are in fact possible, but this is more complicated than simple block allocations.

Under the International Frequency Registration Board's registration process, most radio stations are registered. Some, however, are not, and some are not even operating within the proper allocations. There is nothing the Board can do about this. Whether or not this situation is a problem is a matter of opinion. Clearly states have not so far felt that it is serious enough so that they should take steps through the ITU to alter it, and in certain areas of application, at least, it is unlikely that this attitude will soon change. Article 51 of the Telecommunication Convention explicitly states that "Members and Associate Members retain their entire freedom with regard to military radio installations of their army, naval and air forces."[3] In the realm of civilian activities, however, increasing use of the frequency spectrum may make states more willing to take steps against users who contravene ITU regulations. Short of giving ITU power to impose sanctions, which is most unlikely, there are some things that could be done to work against illicit uses of the frequency spectrum. For instance, the IFRB or ITU staff could be given the power to monitor spectrum usage and publish the findings. Present arrangements allow only national administrations to conduct monitoring activities. The change would be a modest one, but it might slightly inhibit illegal users.

ITU's newer functions relating to the provision of assistance to developing countries can be described in more precise terms than its traditional functions. In its annual summary of its activities for 1968, for instance, the Union reported that it had "through its various programs of technical cooperation, provided assistance to developing countries for a total value of U.S. $ 5,557,688 in the form of 231 expert missions, 274 fellowships implemented or under implementation and U.S. $ 809,800 equipment delivered."[4] The broad goals of these activities were: (a) to promote the development of telecommunication networks in Africa, Asia and Latin America; (b) to strengthen telecommunication services in developing countries; and (c) to develop the human resources required for telecommunication. As has been mentioned, none of these activities are financed from ITU's regular budget, and the bulk of the funds utilized come from the United Nations Development Program.

Evaluating ITU's performance of these newer functions, though, is as difficult as it was in the case of the traditional functions. At the Montreux Conference some representatives of developing states proposed that ITU begin financing technical cooperation activities from its own budget, but this suggestion was rebuffed. Had it been adopted, its effect would have been to give a certain priority to telecommunications. Under the present system states must decide whether the UNDP funds that they might receive should be used for telecommunications or for some other purpose. Few are really willing to take the position that telecommunications should be accorded an absolute priority, and the issue of the adequacy of general development funds, while extremely important, raises matters that go far beyond the scope of this analysis.

The evaluation must then focus on how well ITU performs its activ-

[3] International Telecommunication Convention (Montreux, 1965), Art. 51.
[4] International Telecommunication Union, *Report on the Activities of the International Telecommunication Union in 1968,* Geneva, 1969, p. 36.

ities. There has been no systematic examination of this question. Nor have ITU's efforts been carefully compared with similar efforts conducted by individual governments of developed states or private companies. Impressionistic reports have had both favorable and unfavorable aspects. ITU training enterprises have been said to be more innovative and lively than those that were run under colonial rule by metropolitan powers. They have also been held to be less efficient than those managed by commercial enterprises. Both evaluations, though, may be mainly attributable to the particular projects that were observed rather than to any systematic tendencies. Clearly, this is a subject that needs further investigation. One point, however, can be made. There is little interaction between those elements of the ITU staff engaged in technical cooperation activities and those engaged in its more traditional functions. Undoubtedly the tasks are different, but it is not inconceivable that greater interaction might lead to the formulation of more innovative projects, some of which might have an impact on the feelings of developing states about the Union's traditional functions and the conduct of these states in these functions.

This raises the final point that should be made in describing and evaluating how ITU performs its functions. No other specialized agency of the United Nations has as complex a structure as ITU. How this structure arose is clear; whether it needs to persist is not. It undoubtedly allows special constituencies to be served in special ways by specialists. But one wonders if this purpose could not be served by a more unified structure. Structures, of course, are much less important than the quality of the individuals who fill the posts; good personnel can always surmount awkward structures. ITU's present structure, however, with its elaborate division of authority, is almost an invitation to bickering about picayune matters and may well discourage able personnel from association with the Union. It also tends to compartmentalize the consideration of problems. This may have been appropriate when telegraph, telephone and radio were really quite different, but modern technological developments have made telecommunication systems more and more similar and interdependent. Wholistic treatment is clearly required. Joint groups have been created in ITU, but perhaps the time has arrived for even more far-reaching moves toward unity.

IV

ITU's next Plenipotentiary Conference is scheduled for 1972. The question of institutional reform will surely arise. This issue was raised already at the Montreux Conference in 1965, but the only action taken then was to appoint a study group to prepare a draft constitutional charter. This study group interpreted its mandate as being limited to recommending which sections of the Telecommunication Convention should be placed in a charter that would be permanent and subject to amendment only by special procedure rather than by majority vote at each Plenipotentiary Conference, and which sections should be placed in General Regulations that would continue to be subject to revision at Plenipotentiary Conferences.

The 1972 Conference, then, could conceivably be crucially important to ITU. If in fact a constitutional charter is adopted, it would mean that it would no longer be possible to reconsider ITU's basic mandate and institutional structure at each Plenipotentiary Conference. Undoubtedly this would ease the burden of these conferences. On the other hand, it could mean that ITU's mandate and institutional structure would be firmly set for some years to come, for the experience of the United Nations and the specialized agencies indicates that charters are seldom amended and when they are the changes are minor. With all its disadvantages ITU's present system of reconsidering the entire Telecommunication Convention at each Plenipotentiary Conference may allow greater flexibility.

If this possible flexibility is to be renounced, then it is incumbent on all participants in the 1972 Conference to consider not only how well ITU has performed its functions in the past, but also how adequate the Union is to the needs of the future. Clearly the demand for telecommunication facilities will increase. Communication satellites have opened vast new technological possibilities. At the same time, the less developed states are strongly interested in the rapid development of their economies, and this will involve increased telecommunication facilities. Normal growth in established sectors plus demands stemming from these newer sources are bound to put increased demands on the Union. Perhaps ITU's present institutions are adequate to meet these demands, but it is not unreasonable to suggest that as the Union approaches the twenty-first century, it may need to shed, streamline, modernize and supplement its inheritance from the nineteenth and early twentieth centuries.

Today the performance of ITU's functions is even more vital than it was when the Union was created more than a century ago, and these functions are now much more complex. The absolute amount of telecommunications and the rate of technological change have increased enormously. In view of this, states may well need to reconsider their basic attitudes toward the Union, particularly whether the Union, apart from its technical assistance activites, should be seen principally as a framework within which they can settle matters among themselves by bargaining. No one has suggested that the Union should itself undertake the operation of telecommunication systems or gain coercive powers over states. But several informed observers have questioned the view that the Secretariat's role should be confined to servicing conferences. It is with respect to this issue that serious discussion is needed. Equally serious consideration must be given to the matter of ITU's keeping pace with technological change. Modes of handling problems adopted in an era of less rapid technological change need to be reconibility into ITU's procedures.

In 1865 the states assembled at Paris took a creative and far-reaching step when they formed the International Telegraph Union. That action has enormously facilitated communications among states in the succeeding century. Creative action is also required now to facilitate continued progress.

Chapter 5

INTERNATIONAL CONTROL OF BROADCASTING
PROGRAMS IN WESTERN EUROPE

by *Frits W. Hondius,* The Hague and Strasbourg

I

The purpose of this paper is to examine principles and developments in Western Europe with regard to control over the content of broadcasting programs. Unless otherwise indicated, we shall understand by Western Europe the member states of the Council of Europe: Austria, Belgium, Cyprus, Denmark, the Federal Republic of Germany, France, Greece (which will cease to be a member on December 31, 1970), Iceland, Ireland, Italy, Luxembourg, Malta, The Netherlands, Norway, Sweden, Switzerland, Turkey and the United Kingdom.

The broadcasting process consists of two major components: the technical operation and the production of program content. Control of broadcasting programs may be exercised in different forms. In the context of this paper we take the word "control" in its broadest sense: the establishment of principles, laws, regulations or guidelines governing broadcasting; individual acts and decisions determining the content of programs or the persons who produce them; and the establishment of rules or actions regulating or preventing the emission or reception of broadcasts.

In Western Europe, broadcasting is conceived as a community service. Consequently, all bodies to which broadcasting has been entrusted fall under some form of public control. With some exceptions, broadcasting is a national service, normally taking place within the framework of nation-states. The exceptions are broadcasting by international organizations, such as the European seat of the United Nations in Geneva. But for administrative purposes these broadcasting operations are deemed to take place under the technical responsibility of the host state. Another exception is some pirate transmitters of undefined or ill-defined national origin operating in international waters.

The structure of national broadcasting corporations, their organization, management, financial status, legal status and supervision varies considerably from one European country to the other. These differences are related to the history, legal traditions and national characteristics peculiar to each country. Although broadcasting itself has made a significant contribution to mutual understanding between European nations and toward the elimination of some of the obstacles standing between them, the diversity of Europe must be accepted as a given fact and as a lasting condition. In fact, in the eyes of many people this is a desirable condition. It is one of the sources of international dynamism. The same applies to the world as a whole. Broadcasting should avoid imposing a single vision of the earth to the detriment of richness of cultures.

II

Two issues are of particular importance for the broadcasting pattern: the relationship with the state and the conditions of access to the medium. Although in many European countries broadcasting started as a private undertaking, at an early date it came under various kinds of government control. One reason for this was that the vehicle of transmission belonged to the field of telecommunications, which was already a government service subject to strict national and international regulation and supervision. This accounts, for example, for the rule that no transmitter, whether state or privately owned, may operate without a license issued by those authorities. Another reason is that no government could remain indifferent to the content of radio and television programs. Not only were governments ultimately responsible for the effects of transmissions across the national borders, but they also seized upon radio and television as extremely effective messengers of public policy.

From the outset, radio and television have also been regarded as media of information and expression, and as such their users have claimed freedom of operation. Thus the conflict was born over how to reconcile public control with this freedom. The difference between the press and the cinema, on the one hand, and broadcasting on the other is shown by the problems of choice and access. As far as the freedom of imparting information is concerned, nothing prevents the publication of an unlimited number of newspapers, pamphlets or motion pictures. The limitation of the radio frequency spectrum makes it impossible, however, to establish an unlimited number of radio stations. At the receiving end there are similar limitations. Radio and television audiences are offered a relatively small range of choice, and they cannot "skip pages."

The result of the conflicting requirements of liberty and control has been the establishment of legal regimes giving the state a certain measure of control over broadcasting while recognizing that justice should be done to the diversity of the audiences and to their values and interests in terms of region, language, profession, religion and political convictions. State control in Europe has taken on different shapes, both as regards the control mechanisms (licensing, broadcasting legislation, ownership, staff policy, financing) and controlling bodies (government, parliament, the judiciary). But in no Western European country can the broadcasting service be simply equated with the state administration.

An important difference between the various countries concerns the question of monopoly. Those countries which envisage broadcasting as a unified national service (for example Austria and France) have granted a broadcasting monopoly to one single organization. Audience diversity is expected to be catered to within the national program or by means of regional stations. In other countries the pluralism of the nation is expressed by the broadcasting structure itself (for example Belgium, Germany and The Netherlands). In the case of Germany, the regions form the basis of the diversified structure. Each *Land* has its own autonomous corporation, but functional diversity—politics, religion and the like—is expected to find expression within the bounds of each corporation. The Netherlands exhibits the reverse system; it has geographical unity combined with functional diversity. Broadcasting licenses are distributed among voluntary broadcasting organizations supported by like-minded people (Catholics, Protestants, socialists, humanists) in proportion to their membership. The result is a proliferation of broadcasting corporations, six major ones and a host of small ones, vying for precious transmission time on the three national radio transmitters and two television channels.

The most common model for the legal status of European broadcasting is the public corporation.[1] Its statute is spelled out by a law or charter, but it is functionally independent. The British Broadcasting Corporation has served as a model for many other countries. A second model is that of the French Organisation de la Radio Television Française (ORTF), a semi-state organization (*office*) broadcasting under trusteeship (*tutelle*) of the state but with managerial autonomy.

[1] Debbasch, *Traité du droit de la radiodiffusion* (1967), pp. 51-121.

The third model is that of The Netherlands, where broadcasters are associations or foundations under private law, governed by the legal and fiscal rules of non-profit organizations. A fourth variety is that of the private company. In the case of Radiotelevisione Italiano (RAI), the company is controlled by a government-controlled financial corporation. Sveriges Radio (Sweden) is a state-chartered company the shares of which are divided among the press, certain major national organizations and industry. Finally, Radio Luxembourg, Radio Monte-Carlo and Télé Monte-Carlo are examples of purely private companies, but certain mechanisms safeguard the national interests of the countries involved.

III

No author on the subject has failed to mention the property of radio waves of spanning immense distances. This law of nature has resulted in both intentional and unintentional transmissions across national and political frontiers. Intentional international broadcasting has been practiced by European countries from the very beginning of radio and television. The foreign language programs of the USSR started in the early 1920's. In Western Europe, Italy and Germany followed suit with propaganda broadcasts and Britain, France and Holland with broadcasts to overseas colonies. After World War II, during which international broadcasting was stepped up under the war effort of both sides, external broadcasts became a permanent feature of the system. Apart from the overseas transmissions, expanded inter-European broadcasting and program exchanges in the framework of the European Broadcasting Union and Eurovision reflected the growing integration and mobility of European society in such areas as sports, tourism, migrating workers and economic integration. Commercial advertising was haltingly admitted to the program content as a supplementary source of income for the broadcasting corporations. However, in view of the very modest place they were given among the other program items and in view of protective policies of several countries in favor of their own industries, commercial advertisers explored new and more effective formulas. They identified the privately owned station, transmitting popular music interspersed with ads and occasional news features, as their favored medium.

Since some national broadcasting structures made no provision for this, commercial transmitters have been set up in countries adjoining the target country or aboard ships or artificial structures outside territorial waters. Examples of the first kind are the privately owned radio stations in the periphery of France (Radio Luxembourg, Radio Europe 1 (Saarland), Radio Monte-Carlo or Radio Andorra). Examples of the second type are the floating stations Radio Caroline off Britain, and Radio Veronica off the Dutch coast.

In contrast to Eastern Europe, Western European stations make relatively few foreign broadcasts with political content. The main producer of such programs is Radio Free Europe, which broadcasts from West Germany to Eastern European countries in their own language. It is operated by an American non-profit organization under a license from German authorities.

From the very beginning, broadcasting in Europe has been subjected to international regulation. Analyzing the development of international broadcasting control up to present, we observe that practically all measures of control agreed to among states pertain to the technical process of broadcasting and that the content of programs has only rarely been touched.

One explanation is that international technical cooperation and regulation are indispensable on account of the unlimited possibility of propagation of radio waves across the continent, combined with the limitations of the frequency spectrum which make it necessary to divide the wavebands among states and various categories of users (shipping, aviation, and the like). The two technical limitations just mentioned are of particular importance to Western Europe, which has a heavy concentration of relatively small, highly industrialized and densely populated countries with a rich variety of languages and culture. International technical cooperation is also essential for the further development of transmission technology. It would be impossible to proceed, for example, without international agreement about standards and terminology.

Thus the technical evolution of broadcasting has been accompanied step by step by the setting up of an international controlling machinery and the adoption and codification of rules of international law. This development has been fostered by the fact that broadcasting developed from telegraph communications, which have always been an international carrier *par excellence*. Telegraphy by wire was regulated more than a century ago at the Paris Conference of 1865, resulting in the International Telegraph Convention and the International Telegraph Union. Wireless telegraphy, the next phase in the evolution, was dealt with at the Berlin Conferences of 1903 and 1906 and the London Conference of 1912, the latter resulting in the first set of Radio Regulations. Other milestones were the Conferences of Washington (1927) and Madrid (1932) and the adoption, at the latter conference, of the first International Telecommunication Convention and the creation of the International Telecommunication Union (ITU), which merged the existing radio and telegraph instruments. In 1945 ITU became a specialized agency of the United Nations. Its present terms of reference are the 1965 (Montreux) International Telecommunication Convention and the 1961 Radio Regulations.

The ancestry of ITU as a telegraph organization is visible today in the strict separation it makes between the carrier and the user functions. By limiting itself to the technical aspects and refraining from regulations on program content, ITU has been able to perform its function of worldwide organization and to foster close international collaboration even between countries which are politically opposed.

Now the impelling arguments for technical cooperation and its beneficial results do not apply to program content. The producer of a program can happily go along on his own, as long as the engineers provide him with the technology to transmit his work, and he will in fact be pleased by absence of rules and limitations. One international rule, agreed to by the engineers, has come to his aid: the doctrine of state sovereignty.

IV

During the early stage of development of radio broadcasting, sovereignty in respect to broadcasting was connected with the principle of sovereignty over airspace[2] laid down, for example, by the International Law Association's Conferences of Vienna (1926) and Warsaw (1927). This theory was rather awkward, to say the least, born probably out of ignorance. Not only is it impossible to prevent radio waves of foreign origin from traveling through the airspace above a state, it is also possible—as modern space communications have shown—to establish a link between a state and a broadcasting satellite in orbit far beyond its airspace.

Be this as it may, the rule of sovereignty exists and offers states a latitude of action with regard to their programs. The international lim-

[2] Evensen, "Aspects of International Law Relating to Modern Radio-Communications," *Recueil des Cours* (Académie de la Haye), vol. 2, (1965), p. 526.

itations on sovereignty which states have accepted are of an engineering, not a program content nature. According to the Radio Regulations, no one may operate a transmitter without a license from the government of the appropriate country. This may at first sight seem a confirmation of their sovereignty. In fact it is a limitation in the sense that it imposes a duty upon states and establishes their international responsibility for broadcasting performed by stations under their jurisdiction.

A state that wishes to exercise control over the content of a broadcast of external origin may, in principle, follow any of the following three courses of action. It may try to gain a controlling interest in the production of foreign programs. It may attempt to stop or prevent transmission of an external broadcast to which it takes objection. Or it may attempt to interfere with the reception of such a broadcast.

The latter two actions have been introduced in Western Europe in recent years as remedies against pirate stations operating in international waters. The Netherlands has made use of its powers under the North Sea Installations Act of 1964 to halt a transmitter installed on a platform in the North Sea. Under the British Marine Broadcasting (Offenses) Act of 1967, the British postal service in April 1970 jammed the transmissions of a floating station. In 1965 an international instrument, the European Agreement for the Prevention of Broadcasts Transmitted from Stations Outside National Territories, was opened for signature under the aegis of the Council of Europe. However, these instruments cannot be said to be directed against the *content* of the broadcast but rather against the *fact* of the broadcast itself. This is clear from the wording of Article 1 of the European Agreement—"broadcasts intended for reception or capable of being received"—which makes it rather immaterial whether the broadcast is actually received.

The following grounds have been listed for the control system established by the European Agreement: the international allocation of wavelenghts between states, the registration of frequencies, the prohibition of stations causing harmful interference and government licensing of radio stations. Program content is not mentioned.[3]

In the case of the Dutch and British acts just cited, the declared purpose is to counteract punishable offenses against ITU's radio regulations or against the monopoly of state-licensed stations. The question of program content was indirectly involved, however, in the case of the Marine Broadcasting (Offences) Act. In the public discussion, the government

[3] Green, "Pirate Radio Stations," *Annuaire de l'A.A.A.* (1965), p. 136.

criticized the program policy of the unauthorized commercial stations, which, in turn, argued that they offered entertainment for which there was a demand and which was not available on the regular programs. It should be added that the Agreement and the Acts do not apply to acts commited within the jurisdiction of other states.

In the latter case, only diplomatic action or intervention by force would be capable of gaining control over transmissions at their source. A recent example in Eastern was the seizure of Radio Prague by Soviet troops on August 21, 1968. An example of diplomatic action was the *demarche* made by the Soviet Union with the Austrian government in March 1970 in order to prevent the emission of a television broadcast on the occasion of Lenin's hundredth birthday, to which the Soviet Union took offense. This case showed the dilemma posed by the system combining state responsibility with freedom of expression. The Austrian government, much as it shared the Soviet feelings about the quality of the broadcast, was constitutionally unable to intervene. (It was finally called off for other reasons).

Whitton has examined the problem in the light of pre-World War II relations and has concluded that the state may be held liable for acts of organizations maintained by it or under its actual management or control, and for statements emanating from persons whose acts are to be attributed to its government (for example, a minister).[4]

It is a matter of debate whether the doctrine of state sovereignty may give a state the exclusive right to decide which foreign broadcasts may be received by its own people and to what extent other states should refrain from intentionally beaming broadcasts to other states which do not wish to receive them. The states which uphold this contention base themselves on the principle of non-intervention. In our view, it is doubtful whether a broadcast can be classified under intervention, since the essence of intervention is force or the threat of force. Of course, states which want to bar broadcasts might wish to cite another principle—or rather complex of principles—to which those same states usually adhere: peaceful coexistence. Among the many components ascribed to this principle figures the idea that no country or group of states has the right to impose its system, its *ideas,* upon other peoples. It goes without saying that this principle is of no consequence unless reciprocally observed.

In Western Europe it is not denied that certain types of foreign broad-

[4] Whitton, "Propaganda and International Law," *Recueil des Cours* (Académie de la Haye), vol. 1 (1948), p. 569 at p. 576.

casts may be unwanted from the national point of view, but the grounds and the implications are different from those in Eastern Europe. The major source of friction is a clash between economic interests, for example with regard to commercial broadcasting practiced by peripheral stations or advertisements "accidentally" visible in television broadcasts of sports events. The remedy to these situations is sought in a system of competition rather than elimination. In other words, if external broadcasts produce a noticeable effect in a receiving country, it is an indication of a need of the public to which their own broadcasting system has so far not responded. The remedy, obviously, is to try to introduce adequate provisions in that system.

With regard to television, the situation is slightly more complicated because it is as yet not possible to obtain a broad selection of foreign broadcasts except in border areas. The situation is further complicated by the lack of uniform technical standards of the receiving equipment so that, for example, German broadcasts are visible on the French screens but French broadcasts cannot be picked up by German receivers.

An alternative to the prevention of unwanted external broadcasts at the source is to obstruct their reception by means of jamming. While current opinion under international law does not seem categorically to qualify as unlawful jamming as a protest against certain unwanted radio waves of foreign origin, there is always the chance that jamming may result in harmful interfercene as defined by the ITU Convention. This was suggested, in fact, by a Soviet lawyer speaking at the 1966 meeting of the International Law Association: "It can create harmful interference for the radio services of neighboring countries, not to speak of irrational use of radio frequencies."[5] Other lawyers consider that freedom of information makes any kind of jamming unlawful.[6] We note, incidentally, that this formula does not prohibit states from jamming broadcasts from pirate stations in international waters.

It may be asked whether the principle of satisfactory national service could be invoked to prevent programs from other countries from penetrating. According to the Radio Regulations, stations shall not employ power exceeding what is necessary to maintain economically an effective national service of good quality within the frontiers of the country concerned. Evensen believes that this rule cannot be invoked against the penetration of foreign programs, because it applies particularly to those

[5] *Report of 52nd Reunion, International Law Association* (Helsinki, 1968), p. 212.
[6] Debbasch, *op. cit.*, p. 570.

wavebands which have no long-distance propagation characteristics. Although international freedom of information is not generally recognized, it cannot be said, in Evensen's opinion, to violate any principle of international law.[7]

V

In the foregoing we have examined certain forms of unilateral program control over emissions of external origin. These are rather an exception, and normally unilateral control is confined to regulation and supervision of national broadcasting. We shall now look into the matter of multinational program control.

Since the production of program content in most countries is not a task of the state but of autonomous corporations, international cooperation in this field is also taking place at a non-governmental level. This is one of the reasons for the separation in international control between the engineering and the broadcasting functions and for compulsory regulations in one versus voluntary (contractual) relationships in the other sphere. In 1925 the Union Internationale de Radiodiffusion was created as the international association bringing together national broadcasting corporations. During World War II the Union was dissolved and in 1946 its successor, the Organisation Internationale de Radiodiffusion (OIR), was established in Brussels. Owing to political difficulties between East and West, several Western European corporations refused to join the OIR and founded their own organization, the Union Internationale de Radiodiffusion (UIR). The BBC decided to join neither side. In 1950, eleven Western members resigned from the OIR, which subsequently moved its headquarters to Prague, and together with the BBC they joined the UIR, which was renamed the European Broadcasting Union (EBU).

Shortly afterward, television—a medium eminently suited for Europe's multilingual community—made its entry. Eurovision, established by EBU, became an important multilateral network for the relay of sports, news, entertainment and special events.

Essentially, EBU is a body for international cooperation, not control. The organization facilitates the exchange of radio and television programs between its member organizations. It has never given consideration to securing international control over the content of the programs.

[7] Evensen, *op. cit.*, p. 549.

78

The member organizations of the EBU make their own decisions on program content and they also decide, without interference by EBU, whether or not to offer their programs to foreign broadcasting organizations.

The problem of international control over program content of broadcasting has arisen particularly during the last eight years in connection with the emergence of a new technique of broadcast transmission, the satellite broadcast. This was a new phase in the extension of broadcasting to masses of people, which had set in some ten years earlier with the introduction of the cheap portable radio set. The development of communication satellites for broadcasting has, therefore, been closely followed by UNESCO. This development is proceeding in three stages. The first stage, the putting into operation of stationary satellites for point-to-point communication, has been successfully introduced. The second stage, consisting of stationary distribution satellites for semi-direct broadcasting, is now being introduced. The third stage will consist of broadcasting satellites capable of beaming messages directly to home receivers (augmented or unaugmented) without the intermediary of terrestrial stations.

Lively discussions are going on in the United Nations, UNESCO, ITU and other forums about the implications in international law of direct broadcasting from satellites. For unlike other forms of telecommunications and mass media, which started their development within national or regional structures, space communications are from the very outset a world-wide undertaking which, in accordance with the 1967 Outer Space Treaty, must be based on the peaceful use of outer space for the benefit of all mankind.

At the first UNESCO meeting of space communication experts held in Paris in 1966, several delegations underlined the problems which might arise if their countries were invaded by television programs originating outside and beyond their sphere of influence.[8] The political aspects of this problem were studied in more detail by the Working Group on Direct Broadcast Satellites of the U.N. Committee on the Peaceful Uses of Outer Space. Its report to the General Assembly in December 1969 remarked that no globally accepted rules or adequate international agreements on program content existed. "Nor, considering the diversity of national cultures, would it be a simple matter to develop such principles on a global basis," the report said. "Such agreed principles should be based

[8] UNESCO Doc. MC/52, pp. 11-14.

on respect for national cultures and State sovereignty."[9] Out of the debate in the General Assembly three suggestions emerged. The spokesmen of the Socialist countries stressed the need for protection against misuse of the satellites and pointed out that broadcasts without the permission of the affected states would constitute a violation of their sovereignty and interference in their internal affairs, which they were entitled to counteract. A spokesman for the developing countries counseled avoiding concentrating too much on possible abuses and looking instead to positive measures, such as intensifying regional cooperation. The Swedish delegation proposed the elaboration, through international collaboration, of some sort of generally accepted code of conduct or program standards. This proposal was received with some skepticism in the committee, given the differing views regarding, for example, freedom of speech, censorship and control of media.

It seems legitimate to ask whether the future may bring multinational program production in view of the special problems posed by the broadcasting satellites. Not only will international production be a method to forestall national objections, but it will be unavoidable in view of the huge geographical areas to be covered and the considerable expenditure involved. This applies particularly to Western Europe.

As in the case of radio broadcasting, the engineers have appeared on the scene earlier—or rather, less late—than the future broadcasters. The first initiative was taken in 1962 by the European Conference of Postal and Telecommunications Administrations (CEPT), which looked into the possibilities for a European satellite communications system. For further negotiation the matter was referred to the European Conference for Satellite Telecommunications (CETS). Considering the advanced stage of American and Soviet space technology, CEPT remained on the safe side by not awaiting the uncertain outcome of the independent European space efforts, undertaken particularly by ELDO and ESRO, and it opted for participation in the Intelsat system in 1964. During the years following the first Intelsat agreement, the European countries hoped to catch up somewhat with the two great space powers, but developments have been qualified as discouraging in official European quarters. A CETS conference scheduled for the autumn of 1969, designed to consider a CETS application satellite for Europe to meet the demands of the European Broadcasting Union and by implication to frame a common European position for the Intelsat negotiations, had to be postponed.

[9] U.N. General Assembly, Doc. A/AC. 105/66, p. 9.

The revised target date for the Third European Space Conference was summer 1970. In the meantime, discussions in the CETS committee in London dragged on endlessly, unable to produce a common position. The hesitation of CETS is between continuation of the present structure of Intelsat, or internationalization of Intelsat combined with the admitting of the existence of independent regional satellite systems which would have to be developed through the combined effort of the European technological organizations involved; ELDO, ESRO, CETS, EBU and others. This again is only feasible if overall scientific and technological cooperation can be obtained between Europe's large regional, partly overlapping organizations, the Council of Europe, the European Economic Community, the European Free Trade Association, the North Atlantic Treaty Organization, and the Organization for Economic Cooperation and Development. The basis for such cooperation might be the proposal of the Six of EEC for such cooperation with the Nine of EFTA, as contained in the so-called Aigrain Report.

This bewildering complex of interrelated factors in the field of European hardware cooperation is a foreboding of the problems to be expected in the software sphere. The latter group of problems will be posed on two levels. First, the potential users of satellite broadcasting have to specify and, possibly, pool their wishes and requirements. Next, an organizational framework has to be developed.

In the opinion of the experts, one of the most important fields of application of broadcasting satellites is that of education. To study the feasibility of such application in higher education, a European pilot study has been commissioned by the Council of Europe's Council for Cultural Cooperation, in which the member states of the Council of Europe are participating as well as Finland, the Vatican, Spain and, as an observer, Yugoslavia. This study is to be completed before the end of 1970 so that the results can be presented through the national PTT administrations to the 1971 Administrative Conference of ITU on frequency allocations for satellites.

One of the interesting questions that will have to be studied in this connection is what institutional framework would be employed for the production of common European educational broadcasting programs. Will national broadcasting corporations pool their expertise and broadcasting monopoly for this purpose? Will the users accept the broadcasting corporations as producers? (In Germany, this is a problem of competence between the universities and the broadcasters). Moreover, the question of licensing will have to be considered. The present ITU structure and principles of international radio law base all broadcasting on a national footing. Even a multilateral broadcasting system such as may be created to fulfill the needs of satellite broadcasting would have to be licensed under the laws of a specific state. A working paper submitted to the Committee on the Peaceful Uses of Outer Space has started from the assumption that state sovereignty as well as the system of private enterprise are realities to be reckoned with, so that any pooling should be conducted on the basis of voluntary bilateral or multilateral cooperation.[10]

VI

The approach of the western European countries to broadcasting control should be seen in close conjunction with the development of the relationship between freedom of information and mass media. The cornerstone of the European mass media policies is freedom of information, as laid down in Article 10 of the European Convention of Human Rights of 1950:

"1. Everyone has the right to freedom of expression. This right shall include freedom to hold opinions and to receive and impart information and ideas without interference by public authority and regardless of frontiers. This article shall not prevent States from requiring the licensing of broadcasting, television or cinema enterprises.

2. The exercise of these freedoms, since it carries with it duties and responsibilities, may be subjected to such formalities, conditions, restrictions or penalties, as are prescribed by law and are necessary in a democratic society, in the interests of national security, territorial integrity or public safety, for the prevention of disorder or crime, for the protection of public health or morals, for the protection of the reputation or rights of others, for preventing the disclosure of information received in confidence, or for maintaining the authority and impartiality of the judiciary."

This article traces its ancestry, via the United Nations Universal Declaration of Human Rights of 1948 (Article 19), to the Declaration des Droits de l'Homme of 1789 (Article 11).

The two important implications of the European Convention for broadcasting are, first, that the national system should allow freedom to impart information, and second, that access to information should be given. With regard to the first principle, the Article does not prohibit the state to operate a broadcasting service, but it admonishes states not to refuse access to the medium categorically for certain in-

[10] *Ibid.,* pp. 25-26.

dividuals or groups. "Everyone" may even include commercial companies! With regard to the second principle, it may be suggested that states should not deny their own nationals the right to receive information. It should be noted that the restrictions mentioned in the second paragraph of Article 10 pertain, in fact, not to the freedom to receive information but to the freedom of the broadcasters.

The practical consequence of the acceptance of the European Convention is that it limits the competence of national authorities to exercise program control over broadcasting, and in this sense the Convention is an important instrument of international control. Nationals may cite their own government before the European Commission of Human Rights in Strasbourg for denial of any of their rights with regard to the broadcasting media.

The limitations on the freedom of the broadcasters are founded on the general belief that the mass media are capable of creating undesirable situations in society. The mass media on the one hand disseminate information, broaden horizons, develop taste and knowledge; on the other hand they are capable of manipulation, degradation or alienation.

The fear has been expressed that communication satellites would multiply the benefits and the defects of the mass media a thousandfold. In September 1968, the Consultative Assembly of the Council of Europe convoked a special symposium at Salzburg to clarify the relationship between the mass media and human rights. Though several experts advised the meeting not to overstress the potential dangers posed by the mass media to the individual, the meeting came out in favor of strengthening the protection extended to the individual against undesirable pressures or intrusions by the mass media.

In a resolution (No. 582) of January 13, 1970, the Consultative Assembly recommended modification of the European Convention to secure to the individual the right to seek information and to place a corresponding duty on public authorities to make such information available. The resolution further specified the right of information by stating "There shall be no direct or indirect censorship of the press or of contents of radio and television programmes." These words, in conjunction with Article 10, leave no doubt as to the right of the individual to decide what broadcast of domestic or foreign origin is fit for him to receive.

At the Salzburg symposium, the question was raised whether satellite broadcasts might necessitate a reconsideration of the problem of program content control. The General Rapporteur of the Conference, Lord Kilbrandon, summed up the prevailing European feelings as follows:

> Let us go forward with Mr. Bourquin to 1983, when programmes, he tells us, will be receivable from satellites without relay in every home. No country will make penal laws against the reception of foreign programmes, because they could no more enforce such laws than could Nazi Germany. And we need not think of regulation by international convention. Who would accede to the Russian plea that no broadcast should criticise the Leninist interpretation of Marx? What answer would be given to the primitive savage who wished to protect his family against the American Way of Life? Let us acknowledge here and now that there is no prospect of international agreement on the intellectual or cultural quality of this, or any other mass medium. Everyone will receive what anyone transmits . . .
>
> The time will come when peoples must be plunged into the cold sea of world opinion, and can no longer swim in the warm baths that their governments would prefer them to enjoy.[11]

Yet, uneasy feelings remained in the Consultative Assembly about the forthcoming onslaught upon the European public by the rapid technological development in the field of radio and television, in particular in connection with the development of communication satellites. This concern with protection of the public against the technological and commercial dangers of modern society is concurrently shown in other fields, such as consumer protection and protection of the right of privacy, and new legislative measures founded on internationally agreed principles will no doubt be forthcoming. An indication of this trend is given by a motion for a resolution tabled in the Consultative Assembly on February 18, 1970, which recommends "speedy action by the Council of Europe and all member states" in view of the increased commercialization of the mass media and the risk of undesirable influence upon the cultural level of radio and television programs.

The development of international control of program content of broadcasting in Europe will depend, therefore, on the ability of the users to set up a viable international broadcasting structure. Such a structure should guarantee the possibility of international production of broadcasts in addition to the traditional exchange of national broadcasts.

---

[11] Symposium on Human Rights and Mass Communications (Council of Europe Consultative Assembly) (1967), p. 104.

Chapter 6

PROBLEMS RAISED BY THE CONTENT OF TELEVISION PROGRAMS TRANSMITTED BY TELECOMMUNICATION SATELLITES

by *Roger Errera,* Paris and Reims

I

Three phases are usually distinguished in the development of satellite communications. The first is communication between two fixed points; here a relatively weak satellite broadcasts a signal received from a strong ground transmitter to an extremely sensitive ground receiver. The second phase is that of "distribution" satellites, stronger and capable of serving certain types of receiving stations furnished with special equipment (for a community, a region, etc.) The third phase will be that of very strong satellites transmitting pictures directly to individual receivers.

The first phase has been established for some time. The second and the third will be realized fairly soon, though estimates of just when vary. Whatever the dates and whatever the systems' characteristics, they will cause, everyone now knows, an unprecedented change in communications and telecommunications. They will affect many areas of our collective life and pose innumerable problems for technicians, jurists, sociologists and other specialists to resolve with the cooperation of international organizations and states. The object of this paper is to offer some remarks on the juridical and institutional aspects of the problem of the content of TV programs to be transmitted by communication satellites and on the procedures that may lead to the solution of these problems.

II

The present law of outer space rests on two main sources: texts emanating from the United Nations and other instruments.

The United Nations texts include its Charter, a series of resolutions and a treaty. Several articles in the United Nations Charter can be mentioned here as establishing the essential principles of the international political order. They are the necessity for international cooperation in order to resolve problems of every kind and respect for human rights and fundamental freedoms for all (1:3); the sovereign equality of all United Nation members (2:1); prohibition of United Nations intervention in the domestic affairs of any state (2:7); cooperation in the realms of intellectual culture and education (55b); and finally the existence of different specialized agencies whose programs and activities are coordinated by means of recommendations adopted by the organization (57 and 58).

It is relevant to note here a series of United Nations General Assembly resolutions: No. 1348 (XIII) of December 13, 1958, on the peaceful uses of outer space; No. 1472 (XIV) of December 12, 1959, on international cooperation in the peaceful use of outer space; No. 1721 (XVI) of December 20, 1961, on the peaceful use of outer space; No. 1802 (XVII) of December 14, 1962, on international cooperation in the peaceful use of outer space; No. 1962 (XVIII) of December 13, 1963, declaring the juridical principles which control states' activities in the development and use of outer space; No. 1963 (XVIII) of December 13, 1963, on international cooperation in the peaceful use of outer space; No. 2130 (XX) of December 21, 1965, on the same subject; and No. 2222 (XXI) of December 19, 1966, with regard to the treaty containing the principles which control the activity of states in the field of development and use of outer space, including the moon and celestial bodies.[1]

Regarding other instruments, we shall confine ourselves here to Resolution 4131 of 1966, passed by the Fourteenth Session of the General Conference of UNESCO, which authorized the Director-General to undertake studies of the aspects of space communications that come under that organization's competence and particularly of the agreement establishing a provisional regime applicable to a worldwide commercial system of telecommunications by satellite, signed at Washington on August 20, 1964.

At the present time, the fundamental legal principles of outer space may be summarized as follows:

1. The freedom of use of outer space (Space Treaty, Article 1; Declaration on Outer Space, Sections 1 and 2).

2. The prohibition of national appropriation (Treaty, Article 2; Declaration, Section 3).

[1] These texts are reproduced in the collective work, *Les télécommunications par satellites: Aspects juridiques* (1968).

86

3. The international responsibility of states for their national activities in space whether by governmental or non-governmental organizations (duties of authorization and supervision) (Treaty, Article 6; Declaration, Section 5).

4. The same principle of responsibility as it concerns any damage caused (Treaty, Article 7; Declaration, Section 8).

5. The applicability of international law, of which the Charter of the United Nations forms a part (Treaty, Article 3; Declaration, Section 4).

6. Exploitation in the interest of all, including the idea of public service (Treaty, Article 1; Declaration, Section 1).

Aspects pertaining to the content of broadcasts

The report recently produced by the Working Group on Direct Broadcast Satellites, set up by the Committee on the Peaceful Uses of Outer Space (Resolution 2453 [XXIII] and contained in Document A/AC 105/66 of August 12, 1969), contains the following conclusions. They were reproduced in a report presented on behalf of the Secretary-General of the United Nations at a meeting of government experts on international arrangements in the field of space communications, organized by UNESCO in Paris in December 1969 (COM/SPACE/6). They refer particularly to the problem of broadcast content:

"The Working Group considers that the establishment of an acceptable code for all countries which would regulate the content of direct transmission by satellites raises considerable difficulties, having regard to the different norms which determine, in the different States, the acceptability of programmes; these norms are closely tied to the degree of evolution of the customs and social practices established in each State. However, the Working Group considers that future studies might be developed along the following lines:

Political Questions
The Committee on the Peaceful Uses of Outer Space should continue to examine the political aspects of direct radio transmission by satellites, being guided by the objectives and principles expressed in the Charter of the United Nations, as well as in the resolutions passed by the General Assembly relating to the peaceful uses of Outer Space.

Cultural and Social Questions
The Working Group recommends that *UNESCO* be asked to keep the Committee on the Peaceful Uses of Outer Space informed of all new facts of interest to it, which might crop up in the fields of *UNESCO* competence relating to radio broadcast by satellite, and, particularly, studies and projects relating to education and to the cultural exchanges between countries.
The Working Group recognizes that the question of cultural and social norms incorporated within the framework of national legislations has a bear-

87

ing on questions such as defamation, libel, obscenity, presentation of scenes of violence or horror, the right to safeguard the private life of a citizen, as well a certain number of related problems. It recommends that these questions be studied first by the Committee on the Peaceful Uses of Outer Space, in consultation with *UNESCO* and other competent agencies.

Commercial Aspects

The Working Group considers that in view of the extent of the question in the commercial field, the Committee on the Peaceful Uses of Outer Space should continue the study of this question; information emanating from *UNESCO*, organizations on radio transmission, and other appropriate sources, might be useful."

One might query the validity of the classification proposed by this text. Indeed, the content of television broadcasts embraces one large question in which political, cultural, ideological and economic aspects are closely linked. A broadcast that is politically neutral or inoffensive—supposing that such a neutrality exists and can be verified and that a definition can be stated—could injure a person's private life or a commercial interest. Here are a few examples:

Having reported, on the basis of an AFP [Agence France-Presse] dispatch, that the printers of a provincial newspaper was on strike, an ORTF [Office de la Radio Télévision Française] announcer adds that the newspaper will not appear on the following day. However, on the next day the newspaper appears all the same. The proprietor of the newspaper, considering himself harmed by the incorrect announcement of non-publication, starts a civil action against the ORTF and obtains damages.

One of the German television companies puts on a fashion show in the course of which coats are exhibited. Certain French designs are accompanied by particularly favorable comments. But a coat of German make, is severely criticized. The label on the German-made coat has not, however, been removed and is, for a moment, visible to the viewers. The proprietor of the German house takes out a writ against the television company and obtains damages.[2]

In the same way, publicity prepared for a film, a book or a play can contain, intentionally or not, a certain amount of political propaganda arising from the content of these works and their mode of presentation. However, if it is true that in a great number of states the cultural-social and commercial fields are subject to detailed legislation and regulation while the political field is much less so, it would be inexact to consider that it will always remain so everywhere. Moreover, norms that are not the object of written or public regulation can be as imperative and paralyzing as written regulations.

If, however, one provisionally accepts the U.N. body's classifica-

[2] Catala-Franjou, "Responsabilité civile et pénale pour émissions retransmises par des satellites de télécommunications", *Les télécommunications par satellites: Aspects juridiques*, 1968, p. 196.

tion for the sake of discussion, it seems quite possible to formulate the following remarks.

With reference, first, to any political propaganda which might be contained in a satellite transmission, one should perhaps note that the problem has already been discussed within the framework of the U.N. Several states have offered proposals there like the Soviet Union's that the use of outer space for the spread of war or national hatred not be tolerated. Brazil declared that any propaganda inciting war, class warfare, racial or religious discrimination or any sort of prejudice toward another country should be eliminated from programs broadcast by satellite.

The result of these discussions is contained in the Declaration of 1963 and the Treaty of 1967. The Declaration of 1963 recalls, in its Preamble (sixth line), resolution 110 (II) of November 3, 1947, which condemned propaganda destined to, or of such a nature to, provoke or encourage any threat to peace, any disturbance of the peace, or any aggression.[3] The Declaration considers this resolution applicable to outer space. The Treaty of 1967 restates this resolution in the Preamble (eighth line). According to C. Wilfred Jenks, this test is the result of a compromise between the Soviet wish to include a clause prohibiting the use of outer space for the purpose of war propaganda, national or racial hatred or hostility between nations and the American conception that such clauses were not appropriate for a declaration containing juridical principles.[4] One should note that, up till now, it has not been possible to include the concept of aggression in any international agreement reached through the framework of the U.N. Article 51 of the Charter does not speak of armed aggression. The idea of aggression still persists in the field of information.[5] As for the idea of propaganda destined, or of such a nature, to provoke or encourage any threat to peace, any disturbance of the peace, or any aggression, one should note that several states have already used, for propaganda purposes, radio and television transmissions and unmanned airships entering the atmosphere. According to Catala-Franjou:

> "In 1955, Czechoslovakia complained about receiving pamphlets launched by balloons from the American zone of Germany. Hungary and Poland made the same complaint in 1956, and then Czechoslovakia once again in 1960.

[3] d'Arcy, "L'organisation des Nation Unies et les communications par satellites", *ibid.*, p. 234.
[4] Jenks, *Space Law*, 1965, p. 261.
[5] Schramm, *Satellites de télécommunications pour l'éducation, la science et la culture,* Etudes et documents d'information, No. 53, UNESCO, Paris, 1968, p. 17.

All these incidents were resolved by the mediation of ICAO (International Civil Aviation Organization)."[6]

One should also note that the effectiveness of such propaganda by means of satellite remains questionable and will probably remain so for a long time.[7] Finally, one should note that the idea of propaganda can be, and indeed is, understood differently under different political and ideological systems. A French text by Domenach cites this definition: "Propaganda is an attempt to influence the opinion and the conduct of a society in such a way that the people adopt a predetermined opinion and conduct."[8] The relation of propaganda to publicity on the one hand and to education on the other has still to be defined. The tool of political strategy and, in time of war, of strategy quite simply, propaganda belongs to the political world, national and international, of twentieth century man. Domenach's book discloses a few recent rules: the rule of simplification and enemy number one; the rule of exaggeration and distortion; the rule of overall planning; the rule of transmission; the rule of unanimity and contagion. For all these reasons it is needless to ask if this question of political propaganda will appear in satellite communications.

This problem has also been raised at the international level, beyond the texts already cited. Article 2 of the Geneva Convention signed in 1926 and ratified by more than twenty states, (which, however, do not include the United States or the Soviet Union) declares that the "High Contracting Parties mutually undertake to ensure that transmissions from stations within their respective territories shall not constitute an incitement either to war, against another High Contracting Party, or to acts likely to lead thereto."

A final point should be noted. The texts of 1963 and 1966 already mentioned make recommendations to states and governments. However, television programs are produced in different countries by different types of organizations. Their degree of independence vis-à-vis their governments can depend, among other factors, on the existence of a monopoly conferred by public authority (a monopoly that can apply to transmission as well as to production); on the existence of a private firm coexisting or not with a public organization charged with a public service (but a private enterprise can also be, under certain conditions, charged with public service); on the mode of nomination

[6] Catala-Franjou, *op. cit.,* p. 196.
[7] Almquist and Wiksell, *Communication Satellites,* S.I.P.R.I., 1969, p. 45.
[8] Domenach, *La propagande politique,* 6th ed., 1969, p. 7.

90

of directors; and, finally, on the structure and the composition of the directorate. Such an element can constitute an essential factor in assessing the attitudes of states and their eventual responsibility concerning the political contents of broadcasts by means of communication satellites. Indeed, that is only one example of a fundamental fact that we will have occasion to mention more than once: the diversity of national juridical rules generally dealing with information. Thus Gordon L. Weil remarks that American law makes difficult, if not impossible, any prior control of the American government on any given broadcast.[9]

The commercial aspects of broadcasts and notably the problem of advertising create questions no less delicate to resolve. For one is forced back to the internal regulations controlling television, and these regulations themselves are only the expression of the ideas concerning the place of the methods of information in a society or national culture. The role of advertising in television has been the object of innumerable studies, often critical. In particular, one might mention the Pilkington Commission Report for Great Britain and, for the United States, the report of the Carnegie Commission on Educational Television.[10]

At this point, we will confine ourselves to the following remarks.

The decision to place advertising within television programs is one which, from the commercial and financial point of view, entails evident political and cultural implications. In particular, it is tied to another decision, one to entrust the public service of television to a public organization which benefits from a special budget, whereas the private stations are generally dependent on advertising for their revenue. In Europe, however, more and more of these public organizations entrusted with public service are introducing advertising into their programs. Once advertising is permitted, its role can be conceived in several ways, and particularly its influence on the design and development of programs. In view of the fact that a growing number of countries have authorized television advertising under various arrangements, one may consider such a fact almost irreversible. The United States is, at the same time, the country where television has had the

[9] Weil, *Communicating by Satellite: An International Discussion*, Carnegie Endowment for International Peace and Twentieth Century Fund, New York, 1969, p. 25.
[10] *Report of the Committee on Broadcasting, 1960*, Her Majesty's Stationery Office, London 1962; *Public TV: A Program for Action*, Report of the Carnegie Commission on Educational Television, New York, 1967.

widest development, where advertising occupies a most important role and where projects concerning the use of satellites for transmissions both inside and outside the country are the furthest advanced.

There is a risk of problems arising between countries not having the same attitude or policy toward advertising. A specialist writing on this subject says:

> "It is possible that even an event transmitted by satellite might be, at its origin, "sponsored" in the commercial sense of the term and that it would therefore be a commercial broadcast. Given the differences that exist in the regulation of commercial broadcast between the United States and Europe, it is conceivable that a broadcast that is legitimate at its point of origin might not be so at its destination, the relaying organization not being authorized to broadcast "sponsored" programs; or the product under "sponsorship" might even be banned from television in the receiving country."

The same author continues:

> "Arrangements between a station of origin and the relaying stations in a transatlantic broadcast ought to permit intervention, if the program broadcast includes an advertisement, either to eliminate it, if this is technically possible, or to substitute another advertisement if this is economically desirable."[11]

The *questions of a cultural or social nature* (problems relating to the author's rights will not be studied here) are not the least important ones. The work just cited confirms this:

> "The question of cultural and social norms incorporated into national legislation has a bearing on such questions as defamation, libel, obscenity, presentation of scenes of violence or horror and the right to safeguard the private life of a citizen, as well as a certain number of related questions."

The enumeration of these points leads to the following observations.

For the moment, the protection under both civil and penal law of individuals, collectivities or groups who experience damage as a result of a broadcast transmitted by means of a satellite collides with the diversity of national legislation. This renders the definition of fault and damage extremely difficult and the exercise of lawsuits a very doubtful affair. French law, of course, possesses definitions and a jurisprudence different from those adopted in the Anglo-Saxon countries concerning such concepts as defamation, injury, the protection of privacy and the existence and exercise of the right of reply.

All countries pay particular attention to the protection of children and young persons, which brings into question in relation to the cinema

---

[11] Straschnov, "Quelques aspects juridiques des transmissions de programmes de télévision par satellite", *L'information a l'ère spatiale: Le rôle des satellites de communication,* UNESCO, Paris, 1968, pp. 105-106, 109 (translation supplied).

the classification of films by a public or private control organization or a classification that prohibits people below a certain age from seeing a film.[12] Or again where a film is shown on television, a distinctive notice might be inserted during the broadcast that is not recommended for a young audience.

> "Over and above these juridical considerations, without doubt the direct broadcast by satellite will come up against problems involving national sovereignty and the sensitivity of each country on the cultural level. In passing from one country to another, a documentary can become propaganda; what, for one country, can be a literary masterpiece for another can be an offensive work; and what one country might consider a historical fact might seem a provocation in another."[13]

On this point, it is sufficient to mention the recent and prejudiced character of a European work concerning historical manuals to have an idea of the task yet to be accomplished in the field of television.

In brief, for reasons of a political, social or economic order—and they will often be confused—it is quite possible, even probable, that broadcasts transmitted by communications satellite to all or part of the world will be regarded as undesirable by one or more governments that consider themselves the only qualified judge of the situation. Certainly one can assume, as does Gordon L. Weil, that since the number of broadcasts aimed at a particular region will probably be much greater than those directed at the entire world, it will be easier, given the degree of political and cultural homogeneity, to restrict or eliminate the instances in which the above-mentioned possibilities are likely to arise. Although that argument is accurate enough, such a view perhaps underestimates the importance of the differences, even hostilities that can divide neighboring states. The Middle East, Southeast Asia and Central Europe are good examples.

Beyond cases where broadcasts will be plainly considered undesirable, new juridical problems will certainly crop up. Therefore, one can agree with Straschnov's conclusions:

> "1. At the present stage, where satellites in service are used mainly for the transatlantic transmission of news, juridical problems belong, above all, to public law (access to the ground station and to the satellite) and, to a smaller extent, to private law (problems of defamation and of publicity).
>
> 2. Should future developments (increase in the capacity of present satellites or the launching of new ones) permit the economic use of satellites for the broadcast of artistic programs, the juridical problems will multiply; ques-

---

[12] *Le cinéma et la protection des jeunes,* Council of Europe, 1968 (study by Michard).
[13] Schramm, *op. cit.,* p. 16.

tions concerning authors' rights as well as those of the performing artists will arise.

3. Should the technical development oneday attain the stage of direct reception of satellite broadcasting by the televiewers, a complete recasting of present contracts between television organizations that will want to take advantage of the new transmission methods will become necessary, and states will be obliged to consider the revision of intergovernmental conventions aimed at the protection of broadcasts against commercial exploitation by third parties."[14]

Therefore, we must now consider in what direction and by what methods any kind of solutions might be found to cover all the problems which have just been described.

Toward a Solution

For the sake of discussion, and without pretending that the list is exhaustive, the controlling principles can be stated as follows:

The number and length of the broadcasts by telecommunication satellites will continue to increase in the near future, whatever the statute or organizations controlling the systems (a problem which is presently the object of international negotiations and which will not be considered here). Therefore, the problems raised in the first part of this paper are likely to appear more and more frequently.

The use of outer space for the transmission of television broadcasts by telecommunication satellites must be endowed with the character of a real *international public service*. Accordingly, as the Tenth Symposium on Outer Space held at Belgrade in 1967 by the Institut International de Droit Spatial affirmed:

> "Such a public space service presupposes the existence of an international organization of public law, necessary for the establishment of the appropriate international regulation and to ensure international control; the development of such services could be entrusted to another body or international enterprise by way of concession or by any other method."

Resort to the idea of public service is essential here inasmuch as it involves the application of well-known principles of equality (or non-discrimination), continuity of service, neutrality and the adaption of special interests to the general interest. A more precise examination of these rules, their past application in the area of certain international waterways and their adaptation to the international framework of outer space should be the subject of profound study. A suggestion along these lines was formulated during the United Nations Conference on the Peaceful

[14] Straschnov, *op. cit.*, pp. 110-11.

Uses of Outer Space held in Vienna in August 1968.[15] In a word, what is required here is a new code of good conduct, the principles governing from now on the law of space joining themselves to the imperatives contained in the idea of public service.

The free circulation of information of any kind and of television broadcasts in general can be upheld as a general objective. This liberty ought to take into consideration other rights and implied liberties—for example, the liberty of broadcasting stations; the rights, liberties and interests of individuals and of collective groups of any kind, both in the country transmitting the broadcast and in the country receiving it; and the sovereignty of the states on whose territory the broadcast is received.

Techniques for implementing these principles can either be established within the national framework (and then unilateral action is involved) or within the national framework. On the national level, states have several means of guarding themselves against broadcasts they consider undesirable. The first technique consists of interference (jamming). A second might consist of requiring a state's televiewers to use sets equipped to receive broadcasts only on the approved government frequencies. Unfavorable comment is justified for these methods. There are, of course, the cost and the technical effects of jamming (on neighboring states as well) and the internal and external controls of every kind involved in the second method. But beyond these considerations one must strongly emphasize that such measures contravene the many opportunities open to man through the development of space telecommunications. This does not mean, of course, that the techniques actually used (jamming in the case of radio transmissions) will not be employed or that states will not try to use them against broadcasts transmitted by satellites.

Under these conditions, the choice is easy. It is between coercion and cooperation. As one expert says:

> "Scientific and technical progress and their social use can be impeded or compromised or ... can become dangerous if institutional arrangements are not undertaken immediately to make them acceptable to the community of states and to make sure that they will serve the common good. Accordingly one must state the dilemma bluntly. In order to resolve this problem, there is room for only two methods: force or law, coercion or international cooperation. Coercion means interference arbitrarily imposed, the destruction of transmission equipment and the prohibition of manufacture, importation or even the possession of receiving equipment. On the juridical level, cooperation represents the search for international agreement and international re-

---

[15] See also Kiss, "La Conférence des Nations-Unies sur l'utilisation pacifique de l'espace", *Annuaire français de droit international*, 1968, pp. 756-760.

95

gulations acceptable to the states and, through them, the organizations for producing and diffusing space information together with a discipline, a natural responsibility to prevent abuse and injury of any kind to collective and legitimate private interests in every national community."[16]

It is within the international framework that, from every point of view, the most satisfactory solutions can be sought. Several systems are available. Gordon L. Weil asks that countries capable of launching satellites prohibit their use to those countries whose broadcasting organizations might transmit programs which are unacceptable to other countries, and to abstain themselves from such practices. Weil asks also that agreement be reached between countries and stations, on the one hand, and their neighbors on the other, on what might be acceptable broadcasts.

A second system would demand the prior agreement of each country before a broadcast. A variant achieving the same result would consist in making acceptance the rule, the right of veto always being available.

In a third system, the radio-television organizations would develop between them mutually acceptable rules concerning the contents of the broadcast programs, and the rules would eventually be incorporated into a convention.

Discussion

The technique of international agreements (multilateral or bilateral) is the one that has been the most frequently employed up to now, from the international conventions that created the International Telecommunication Union to the Washington Agreement of 1964 and the agreements that followed. These forms are known, as are the results. So far as the question we have been studying is concerned, perhaps the limitations of the method have not been clearly perceived. Commenting on the present situation, in which, from the European point of view, the directorates of mail and telecommunications "believe that they themselves have the right to decide if the message to be televised is sufficiently important to justify a halt in telephonic and telegraphic traffic at the busiest hours of that traffic," Straschnov correctly states:

> "This particular form of "censorship," instituted in the guise of a necessarily restricted access to satellites and presaging, in that case, other modes of the "right to see" under intercontinental broadcasting will eventually pose broadcasters (for reasons that need not be purely technical) a very serious problem

[16] Terrou, *Coopération internationale pour l'utilisation des communications spatiales à des fins d'information, d'éducation et de culture,* UNESCO, Paris, 1965, p. 9.

96

and will call for an equitable solution, failing which the use of satellites for television will be limited to extremely exceptional events."[17]

Concerning the future, is it normal, and in line with the spirit of a public international service and with the norms established up to now to rely solely on agreements between governments either to obtain permission to transmit a program or to develop further the general rules governing broadcasting and its contents? It is doubtful. At a moment when economic barriers are disappearing or weakening in the world, it would be highly paradoxical to see the most recent and powerful means of communication between men become the ultimate haven of unlimited national sovereignty and of cultural or ideological protectionism. This would truly be a backward step. For this reason the second technique is preferable: for radio-television organizations to develop themselves, by regular contact and exchange of acquired experience, the rules of conduct relating to program content. Such a procedure offers the following advantages.

It is already practiced, in a sense, within the regional framework (in the European Broadcasting Union, among others) with good results.

It meets an unquestionable need: the autonomy of the radio-television organizations with respect to the public authority in the development of general policy and particularly in establishing program contents and relations with foreign organizations.

In the international field, as in the national, we are passing from a period of scarcity, and therefore of access limited, controlled and distributed by states, to a period of increasing abundance, and therefore of pluralism and autonomy.

The implications of such change are fundamental, and it is probable that they will become still more numerous.

If the last of the techniques described here is adopted two questions of differing importance will remain to be resolved in addition to the basic problems considered in the first part of this paper. All television organizations do not possess the same legal basis or even a comparable basis. One country gives a monopoly to a single public enterprise, in another an independent public service coexists with a private enterprise subject to certain obligations of public service, in another private organizations compete under the regulation of a government office. It is therefore to be expected that these differences in authority and situation will cause differences in behavior and attitude in the field of our study. Despite its importance, this fact must *not* be considered as an obstacle,

[17] Straschnov, *op. cit.,* pp. 104-105.

and it would be all the less permissible to await some hypothetical accommodation of statutes (which, moreover, nobody wants) since time is pressing and solutions must be found immediately. Additionally, as regular contacts are established between these organizations, the frequency and habit of treating in common the same problems will gradually create methods and the outlines of solutions acceptable to the majority among them. Neither must one forget that when questions of a truly political nature arise, as they will, it would be difficult to keep governments from handling their responsibilities as they have done up till now.

The special United Nations Committee on the Peaceful Uses of Outer Space would be the best agency to organize regular contacts between radio-television organizations and to be the starting point for future regulation and understanding. During the Vienna Conference, the representative of the Secretary-General of the United Nations suggested that the possibilities offered by the existing international institutions be used from now on and that, in particular, the facilities and structures of the United Nations be strengthened in this perspective.

Will the development of these common rules have to be embodied in an agreement at some given time? The question is probably premature and of secondary importance at that. Not to wait to take advantage of experience and to press for a written convention would risk the establishment of rules that were either too vague or too detailed. The choice would then lie between uselessness and paralysis. Domestic experience in fields where such codes exist (for example, cinema in the United States, televised advertising in France) does not help and does not permit the formation of any *a priori* conclusion since the contexts are so different, and in satellite communications the problems are entirely new. At least one can formulate the opinion that it is preferable not to hamper such new phenomenon with a chain of regulations whose strict application would be so uncertain. In the international field, as in the national, legislative "inflation" is rarely a sign of health.

Chapter 7

EAST-WEST COOPERATION IN SPACE TELE-
COMMUNICATIONS: A SOCIALIST COUNTRIES' VIEWPOINT

by *Vladimir Kopal,* Prague

The scientific and technological revolution of our time undeniably presents some attractive prospects for our generation. New fields of activity are being opened, new environments are becoming accessible to mankind. Soon we shall have at our disposal more powerful means and
resources than ever before to tranform, step by step, the lives of individuals as well as whole nations.

The progress of space exploration is characteristic of the achievements
of contemporary science and technology; the successful development of
space telecommunications represents one of its most significant applications and one that has already brought practical benefits. The increasing
influence that this development will have on communication among
nations needs to be carefully followed and studied by those who are interested in international relations and the regulation thereof by international law.

The main legal instrument governing the activities of states in outer
space is the Treaty of January 27, 1967.[1] Surprising as it may seem,
this document does not include any principle that explicitly applies to
the legal aspects of space telecommunications. Certain provisions, especially those stated in Article 1 and the aims expressed in the Preamble,
are applicable to the establishment and operation of space telecommunications systems and the spread of information via satellites. But no
generally binding instrument of space law setting forth principles and
rules of international law concerning specific aspects of telecommunications has yet been adopted.

---

[1] Vereshchetin, "Basic Principles of Space Law," *Soviet Year-Book of International Law* (1966-1967), pp. 116-126; Kopal, "The Space Treaty of January 27, 1967
and Related Problems," *Studies in International Law,* Prague, 13 (1968): 97-138.

Recommendations of the U.N. General Assembly Relevant to Space Telecommunications

Relatively early in the development of space telecommunications the United Nations General Assembly drew the attention of the world community to the emerging problems of this field. In its Resolution 1721 (XVI) of December 20, 1961, the General Assembly recommended certain principles for the guidance of nations in the exploration and use of outer space and initiated the development of international cooperation in this field. The General Assembly also unanimously adopted certain recommendations concerning a number of issues raised by the anticipated growth of space telecommunications.

In part D of the Resolution the General Assembly expressed its belief that "communications by means of satellites should be available to the nations of the world as soon as practicable on a global and non-discriminatory basis." At the same time it stressed "the need to prepare the way for the establishment of effective operational satellite communication."

In the same Resolution the General Assembly also addressed a series of recommendations to the International Telecommunication Union, which was just preparing its Extraordinary Administrative Conference on Radiocommunications scheduled for 1963, and to other specialized agencies and bodies, asking them to pay due attention to some specific aspects of space telecommunications.

On several subsequent occasions the General Assembly has returned to consideration of those problems, declaring that "communication by satellite offers great benefits to mankind as it will permit the expansion of radio, telephone and television transmission including the broadcast of United Nations activities, thus facilitating contact among the peoples of the world." The General Assembly has also emphasized "the importance of international cooperation to achieve effective satellite communications which will be available on a world-wide basis.[2]

Unfortunately, although these invitations and requests were unanimously adopted, they were legally nothing more than recommendations, and therefore failed to surmount the differences in intentions and plans between the two major space powers.

As early as 1962 a semi-private corporation for the commercial use of space telecommunications was established in the United States, and in 1964 the United States and other Western countries sponsored the Inter-

[2] Resolution No. 1802 (XVII), Dec. 14, 1962, Part 4.

im Arrangements for a commercial telecommunications satellite system. The Socialist countries of Eastern Europe did not participate in this venture, although the Soviet Union and the United States signed a bilateral agreement providing for some degree of cooperation in the field of space telecommunications.[3] On April 23, 1965, the Soviet Union successfully started its own program by launching its first Molniya satellite almost simultaneously with the launching of the U.S. satellite Intelsat 1.

In its Resolution No. 2222 (XXI) of December 19, 1966, the U.N. General Assembly commended the text of the Space Treaty and proposed the study of questions relative to "the utilization of outer space and celestial bodies including the various implications of space communications" (a proposal repeated in subsequent Resolutions Nos. 2260 (XXII), 2453 (XXIII) and 2601 (XXV). By that time the issues had become more complex than they had seemed only a few years before. Taking into account new trends in telecommunications, the U.N. General Assembly did not hesitate to urge the Committee on the Peaceful Uses of Outer Space to study and report on the technical feasibility of communication by direct broadcast from satellites, the current and foreseeable developments in this field and the implications of such developments.

In addition to direct broadcasting from satellites, which will, in the not too distant future, substantially increase the spread of information throughout the world,[4] the special interest of developing nations in the use of space communications has provided further impetus to study of this field. Their interest may compensate for the present concentration of world telecommunications power in the two superpowers, the United States and the Soviet Union, and in Western Europe, and encourage the growth of a truly global network, one that would cover the whole world including developing countries themselves.

These facts, needs and expectations were made evident in the U.N. Conference on the Exploration and Peaceful Uses of Outer Space held in Vienna in 1968. The concerns of this conference included "the practical benefits of space programs on the basis of scientific and technical achievements, and the opportunities available to non-space Powers for international co-operation in space activities, with special reference to the needs of the developing countries".[5]

[3] See the Agreement signed between the USSR Academy of Sciences and NASA on June 8, 1962 in Geneva, and related documents, published in *Yearbook of Air and Space Law* (1965), p. 502.
[4] See United Nations, Committee on the Peaceful Uses of Outer Space, *Report of the Working Group on Direct Broadcast Satellites* (A/AC.105/51).
[5] United Nations, General Assembly, Resolution No. 2221 (XXI) of Dec. 19, 1966,

But the most important stimulus to the concern of the international community in telecommunications today is the speedy development of space communications technology itself and the fact that a crucial moment has been reached in the establishment of space telecommunications systems.

For at the beginning of the 1970's, space telecommunications moved out of its initial stage of development, the demonstration of its ability to compete with traditional means of telecommunications, and proceeded to a new stage of definitive organizational build-up in the interests of further development to satisfy growing communications needs. At this point the nations of the world, and especially the two major space powers, have to make a key decision: either to join their efforts and, surmounting their deep conflicts in concepts of property and philosophies, establish one space telecommunications organization based on principles acceptable to all, or to tolerate the coexistence of two or more space telecommunications systems with all the inevitable political, technical and financial consequences of multiple systems.

Characteristics of the Present Organization of Intelsat and some Trends in Its Further Development

The scientific and technological achievements of the United States in the field of space telecommunications since the very early years of astronautics unquestionably deserve admiration as contributions to telecommunications and communication among the nations of the world in general. On the other hand, the existing organization whose purpose is to utilize those achievements, Intelsat (the International Telecommunications Satellite Consortium),[6] includes, in our opinion, a number of substantial weaknesses which, unfortunately, are not likely to be completely repaired in the definitive organizational framework discussed in 1969 and 1970.

A number of criticisms addressed to Intelsat have been published in various statements and papers during the past few years, in both the East and the West. Those criticisms that are connected to the subject under consideration should be recalled here.

The first is the lack of universality, the fact that Intelsat membership

and *Report of the Committee on the Peaceful Uses of Outer Space* (A/7285), 1968, p. 16 s.
[6] Charyk, "Commercial Communications Satellites"; Johnson, "Organization and Activities of Intelsat," *Papers presented to the U.N. Conference on the Exploration and Peaceful Uses of Outer Space, Vienna, August 14-27, 1968.*

is not open to all the nations of the world. Certainly, the Agreement Establishing Interim Arrangements for a Global Commercial Communications Satellite System, signed in Washington in 1964, recalled in its Preamble the above-mentioned principle of the General Assembly Resolution No. 1721. It stated that:

> "Satellites communications should be organized in such a way as to permit all States to have access to the global system and those States so wishing to invest in the system with consequent participation in the design, development, construction (including the provision of equipment), establishment, maintenance, operation and ownership of the system."

In reality, however, the Agreement has remained open only to nations that are members of the International Telecommunication Union. And although this specialized agency includes a large number of nations it has not yet agreed upon the representation of such nations as the German Democratic Republic, North Vietnam, North Korea and the People's Republic of China, in spite of the fact that West Germany, South Vietnam and South Korea have been admitted. And the present membership of Intelsat represents only about half of the members of ITU.

Recent discussions of the definitive arrangements for Intelsat have tended to favor keeping the present prerequisite of ITU membership, although in a modified form which would probably authorize a qualified majority of a newly reformed Assembly to admit other applicants or provide direct or indirect access to the satellites of the system for non-members.[7]

The persistence of the ITU clause is surprising in view of the trends in contemporary international law reflected in most important East-West agreements since the Moscow Test Ban Treaty of 1963, including the Space Treaty and the Agreement on Assistance to Astronauts. All those instruments have been open for signature or accession to all nations without discrimination.

The second objection, which is actually a whole complex of objections, concerns the position of members within the Intelsat structure. These objections refer particularly to eligibility for, and representation on, the present Intelsat governing body, its decision-making and, probably most clearly, its managing body. All of these aspects of Intelsat's governance guarantee a dominant position for one nation or, to use the precise terms of the U.S. Communications Satellite Act of 1962, for

---

[7] Report of the Interim Communications Satellite Committee on Definitive Arrangements for an International Global Communications Satellite System, Plenipotentiary Conference, Washington, Doc. 6, Jan. 15, 1969, p. 44; Doc. Com. 1/94, March 15, 1969.

"a private corporation," subject "to the provisions of this Act and, to the extent with this Act, to the District of Columbia Business Corporation Act."

Even those commentators who are willing to recognize the positive work done by Intelsat share the view that, "as a matter of principle, it is not admissible that the manager of Intelsat be at the same time a member of the governing body and also a national corporation," and that "there is no reason why a global system should be the property of a sole organization; that would constitute a monopoly."[8]

It should be recalled that the definitive arrangements will probably require some substantial amendment to the present structure of Intelsat. Specifically, a system of three bodies—that is, an Assembly, perhaps with a representation of all members; a Governing Body of limited size; and a Management Body of more or less international character—will probably be introduced.

Some Intelsat members strongly oppose the present distribution of voting power according to which "any one representative or combination of three representatives having the largest voting shares on the Governing Body [is] able to prevent or impose a decision of the Governing Body solely because of the casting of its votes or their votes." Nevertheless, the principle of weighted voting in the most important organ will very probably be maintained. Likewise, it is not yet clear whether or to what extent demands "that the Organization have a permanent international Management Body under the authority of a Director-General who would be directly subordinate to the Governing Body" and that "all posts in the Management Body shall be open to qualified personnel of the Participating States, with the aim of securing the highest degree of efficiency"[9] will result in removal of the monopolistic powers of the present manager.

It is not necessary here to analyze in greater detail how the existing structure of Intelsat is reflected in other more specific provisions of the Washington Agreements of 1964 and also in the Supplementary Agreement on Arbitration signed in 1965.[10]

[8] Comments made by Voge in discussions on the IISL *Tenth Colloquium on the Law of Outer Space,* September 24-29, 1967, Belgrade (*Proceedings,* p. 70).
[9] Report of the Interim Committee cited in note 5, pp. 63 and 66.
[10] See the critical comments in the paper of V. S. Vereshchetin, "Legal Questions of Satellite Telecommunications," at the Washington Intelsat Conference, delivered at the Twelfth *Colloquium on the Law of Outer Space,* Mar del Plata, 1969.

The fact that the Socialist countries have not become members of Intelsat does not mean that they have no interest in the development of new means of communication by telecommunication satellites. Since 1965 the USSR and eight other socialist countries have worked together in different branches of space exploration involving the construction of space objects to be launched into orbit by means of Soviet rockets. This cooperation, referred to as Interkosmos, includes research on peaceful uses of telecommunications satellites for which the successful launchings of Soviet Molniya satellites as well as the construction of the USSR telecommunication system Orbita[11] have created a concrete base.

A comparison of Soviet and American space programs shows that their aims and trends are not completely parallel. Moreover, the telecommunications needs of the Soviet Union and other socialist countries differ from those of the United States and many other Intelsat members, due to geographical conditions and the intensity of their mutual relations. On the other hand, Soviet space programs have not been guided by commercial interests as the establishment of Comsat and the arrangements concerning Intelsat have.

At a meeting held in Moscow, April 5-13, 1967, a consultative group of experts from Bulgaria, Czechoslovakia, Cuba, Hungary, Mongolia, the German Democratic Republic, Poland, Rumania and the USSR prepared a document proposing the establishment of an international satellite communications system for transmission of TV programs, telephone calls, and other kinds of information. Even in its earliest stages the proposal emphasized the open character of the future system, accepting the participation of all nations willing to join it.[12] On August 5, 1968, a Draft Agreement on the Establishment of an International Communications System Using Artificial Earth Satellites was transmitted by the representatives of eight Socialist countries that are members of the United Nations to the U.N. Secretary-General and through him to

[11] At present, the Orbita system has at its disposal a network of more than 20 ground stations which covers the whole territory of the USSR and permits broadcasting of TV programs to distant regions of Siberia, the Northern Territories, the Far East and Central Asia. The system is also used for the spread of news, meteorological maps and telegraphical and telephonic communications. *Septième rapport de l'Union internationale des télécommunications sur les télécommunications et les utilisations pacifiques de l'espace extra-atmosphérique*, Geneva, 1968, p. 90.
[12] U.N. Doc. A/6668, May 10, 1967.

the Committee on the Peaceful Uses of Outer Space.[13]

Article 1 of the draft agreement provides for the establishment of a new international communications system as well as an international organization called Intersputnik.

The technological aspects of the Intersputnik structure would be similar to those of Intelsat.

The system would consist of two components. The first would include the communications satellites and the relay transmitters and on-board equipment necessary for their operation as well as the ground systems for satellite control, telemetry and other ground operations. This component would be the property of Intersputnik or would be leased from organization members that have such systems.

The ground stations themselves would be the property of the nations which constructed them in their respective territories.

The launching and emplacement of satellites in orbit would be carried out by those members of the organization possessing the necessary facilities, on the basis of bilateral agreements between the organization and such members.

The document also includes a number of principles concerning the assignment of communications channels both to members of the organization and to other users in accordance with the provisions of the agreement; the legal personality of the organization, which would enjoy in the territory of its members the legal capacity to carry out its functions and achieve its purposes; and last but not least, coordination with ITU and other international organizations, governmental agencies and non-governmental entities using telecommunication satellites, in both technical aspects (the use of frequency spectrum, the application of technical standards to communications channels and equipment standards) and international regulation. Those principles, confirming the need for international cooperation with other relevant bodies and indicating a suitable basis for its development, characterize the intentions of the sponsors of the agreement, who are far from claiming any exclusive or discriminatory position for the new organization. They take into account practical issues arising from the coexistence of two or more space telecommunication systems, and they recognize the functions of the International Telecommunication Union.

The most significant difference between the organizational principles of Intersputnik and those of Intelsat concerns administration and decision-making. The draft agreement of Intersputnik provides for two or-

[13] U.N. Doc. A/AC. 105/46, August 9, 1968 (translation from the Russian).

gans, a Council of representatives of members of the organization, which would be its governing body, and a Directorate, which would serve as a permanent executive and administrative organ, headed by a Director-General. Of course, as is usual in other international organizations, the Council might establish such subsidiary organs as might be necessary to achieve the purposes of the agreement.

The internal structure of the organization as well as its decision-making would be governed by traditional principles of international law based on the legal equality of all its members. Each member would be represented and have one vote in the Council, which would meet in regular sessions annually. The Council could also hold special sessions on its own initiative or at the request of the Director-General or any member of the organization, subject to the agreement of not less than one-third of the members. Council decisions would be adopted if they received not less than two-thirds of the votes of the Council members, and two-thirds of the total membership would constitute a quorum. Nevertheless the Council would endeavor to take its decisions unanimously.

The draft agreement sets forth the Council's functions in both general terms (it would be empowered to consider "any questions covered by the Agreement") and specific provisions for its most important activities. These functions include adoption of measures for the establishment and operation of the space complex and satellite control systems; consideration of plans for further development and improvement of the communications system; consideration and approval of a satellite-launching program as well as the laying down of technical standards for satellites; approval of a plan for the allocation of communication channels among members of the organization, as well as of the procedure and conditions for the leasing or use of channels by non-members; election of the Director-General and his deputy and supervision of the work of the Directorate; approval of the regulation, structure and establishment of the Directorate as well as its plans for each calendar year; consideration of the annual reports of the Directorate in its work; consideration and approval of the budget of the organization; determination of amounts and dates of payment of contributions to be paid by the governments of the organization's member nations, as well as determination of the financial and technical conditions for the admission of new members of the organization; establishment of the rate for transmission of a unit of information or the cost of leasing a channel; consideration of proposals for amendments to the agreement and submission thereof to members of the organization for their approval.

The draft agreement also describes in detail the role of the Directorate. The executive organ would consist of a Director-General, his deputy and the staff needed by the organization. The Director-General would be the principal administrative officer of the organization and would represent it in its relations with its members concerning all questions related to its work and relations to international organizations with which the Council would consider it necessary to cooperate. The Director-General would be responsible to the Council for the work of the Directorate and would perform all of the executive functions enumerated in the draft agreement. The Director-General and his deputy would be elected for a term of four years and might be re-elected. The staff of the Directorate would be recruited from among citizens of the organization's member nations, with due regard for their professional competence and the principle of equitable geographical representation.

For its financing the organization would set up a basic fund to cover the expenses of scientific research and experimental and design work on communications satellites and ground stations; the design, construction, acquisition or leasing of the space complex; the charges for launchings and emplacement of satellites in orbit; and the acquisition or leasing of ground control systems.

The organization's administrative expenses would be covered by a special fund set up simultaneously with the Directorate.

In principle, each member of the organization would contribute to both funds in amounts proportionate to its use of the communications channels. If in the course of designing and creating the communications system it should become necessary to increase the fund, such additional expenditure would be distributed among those members adopting such a decision. In the event of the admission of new members to the organization, or the withdrawal of any members from it, the scale of assessments would be adjusted accordingly. Contributions to the funds of the organization would be made in transferable rubles or in freely convertible foreign currencies.

Income derived from the operation of the telecommunications system would be distributed among the members of the organization initially to reimburse them for expenses connected with the cost of the outer space complex, the launching of communications satellites and the cost or rental of satellites and ground control systems; the balance of such income would then be distributed among the members of the organization in proportion to the amounts of their contributions.

The draft agreement provides for the distribution of communications channels among members of the organization on the basis of need. If the number of channels available were more than enough to meet the combined needs of all members, the additional channels might be leased to non-members. The Council would fix the rates of payment for their use.

The draft agreement also supports the right of any member to withdraw from the organization, and describes the amount and manner of monetary compensation due to any member withdrawing from the organization. It also includes a provision concerning total or partial suspension of rights deriving from membership in the organization upon a decision of the Council, as well as provisions concerning the dissolution by agreement among its members.

Although the definitive text of the agreement on Intersputnik will only emerge from the deliberations of a future conference with the participation of those governments which decide to become its members, the main features of the above-mentioned principles will very probably remain without substantial changes. As one observer has noted:

> "The proposed scheme permits honest and equal cooperation among the nations that would establish the international organization. It will be an organization without privileged and unequal partners, in which the possibilities of using the latest achievements of science and technology are guaranteed to each participating State."[14]

The Role of International Organizations in Establishing a World Satellite Telecommunications Service.

The coexistence of space telecommunications systems will probably not remain limited to two entities. A Western European system might become the third partner in the game, and some additional, national systems may also be established.[15]

Under those conditions the alternative of coexistence of two or more telecommunications systems should be shaped so as to lead to the establishment of a worldwide telecommunications service by coordination, cooperation, and interconnection of the several systems, be they of a global or of a more limited character.

At its 1967 Colloquium in Belgrade, the International Institute of

[14] Lukin, *Legal Aspects of the Use of Artificial Satellites for Purposes of Meteorology and Telecommunication* (in Russian), Moscow, 1970, p. 135.
[15] Compare Pépin, "Comment concevoir l'organisation internationale mondiale future des télécommunications par satellites," *Les télécommunications par satellites: Aspects juridiques,* CNRS, Paris, 1968, p. 293.

Space Law, which had been considering legal problems of telecommunications satellites every year since 1965, adopted the following conclusions:

1. Satellite telecommunications constitute an international public service.

2. Such a service requires the existence of an international organization of public law to adopt appropriate international regulations for international control. Development or exploiting services might be assigned to another entity or international enterprise by concessions or in some other way.

3. It is desirable that, within the framework of a world satellite telecommunications system, regional or continental systems be established with satellites to be owned directly by the interested states.

4. The arrangement of a world organization for satellite telecommunications might involve either the extension of the attributes and functions of existing international organizations (for example, the International Telecommuncation Union) or the establishment of a new international organization.[16]

In a similar spirit, at its 1966 meeting in Helsinki, the International Law Association asked its Committee on Space Law to consider the problems of an "international organ dealing with questions relating to the establishment and exploitation of a telecommunications satellite system (or systems)," thought it was not able at the time to decide without additional studies whether such a role should be filled by a new, independent international organization or a section of an existing organization.[17]

It is indisputable that, in the present situation, ITU might and should assume this role, for ITU is an established international organization with long experience and many members. Moreover, the problem of telecommunications has to be considered as a whole, in connection with the traditional modes of telecommunications. In many of its resolutions concerning peaceful uses of outer space the U.N. General Assembly has addressed a whole series of recommendations concerning space telecommunications to this specialized agency.

Over the past few years, in its coordinating and regulating functions, ITU has dealt with urgent issues in satellite telecommunications. For example, at its Administrative Conferences in 1959 and 1963, ITU

[16] *Proceedings of the Tenth Colloquium on the Law of Outer Space,* pp. 71-72.
[17] *Report of the Fifty-Second Conference, International Law Association,* Helsinki, 1966, p. XX.

allocated a part of the frequency spectrum to space services and adopted a list of definitions relating to space telecommunications.[18]

At its Twenty-third Session, on May 11-23, 1968, the ITU Administrative Council considered the role which ITU should play in the field of space telecommunications and adopted Resolution No. 632 concerning convocation of the World Administrative Conference on Space Radiocommunications, which is to be held in 1971. At the same time the Administrative Council emphasized, in Resolution No. 637, ITU's fundamental purpose, as outlined in Article 4 of the Montreux Convention, "to maintain and extend international cooperation for the improvement and rational use of telecommunications of all kinds" and "to promote the development of technical facilities and their most efficient operation with a view to improving the efficiency of telecommunication services, increasing their usefulness and making them, so far as possible, generally available to the public."

It may be asked whether ITU's traditional and current position is adequate to the anticipated demands on a world telecommunications organization in the period of coexistence of developed satellite communications systems. From many sides a number of new poblems have been pointed out to which almost no attention has been paid so far and for the consideration of which ITU, in its present condition, does not seem prepared. The list of problems includes such obvious difficulties as, for example, the existence and operation of military systems, which are considered exempt from ITU regulations.[19]

The extended use of telecommunications satellites raises a number of educational and cultural problems, which are being studied by the United National Educational, Scientific and Cultural Organization. This specialized agency convened, as early as December 1965, a meeting of experts "to advise on a long-term program to promote the use of space communication as a medium for the free flow of information, the spread of education and wider international cultural exchanges."[20]

In February 1968 UNESCO organized a meeting of representatives of regional broadcasting unions which recommended convoking an as-

---

[18] Reprinted in Jenks, *Space Law* (1965), p. 331. See also ITU, *Radiocommunications in the Exploration and Peaceful Uses of Outer Space* (U.N. Doc. A/CONF. 34/I. 16).

[19] Estep, "Some International Aspects of Communications Satellite Systems," *Proceedings of the Conference on the Law of Space and Satellite Communication*, Washington, 1964, p. 177.

[20] *Communication in the Space Age: The Use of Satellites by the Mass Media*, UNESCO, 1968.

sembly of experts on an intergovernmental level to define the substance of international agreements corresponding, in the field of space communications, to the main objectives of UNESCO, and drafting a declaration of principles governing the uses of space communications for peaceful purposes.

Although the value of this last suggestion is indisputable, it seems to exceed the scope of activities of a specialized agency such as UNESCO. The United Nations itself is better qualified to perform such a task. For this reason the Czechoslovakian delegation at the Seventh Session of the Legal Subcommittee on the Peaceful Uses of Outer Space proposed to discuss the elaboration of the legal principles on which the creation and functioning of space communications should be based.[21]

The aim of the Czechoslovakian initiative has been both to declare that all activities of satellites telecommunications systems, including direct broadcasting, qualify as space activities governed by principles of space law (including the principle of the responsibility of states) and to prevent space telecommunications systems from becoming instruments of war propaganda and international tension.

The elaboration and adoption of such an instrument would, I suggest, be a contribution to the development of cooperation among nations in telecommunications, to their better communication with each other and to their mutual understanding generally.

[21] *Report of the Committee on the Peaceful Uses of Outer Space* (U.N. Doc. A/ 7285), p. 135.

Chapter 8

THE CONTRIBUTION OF TELECOMMUNICATIONS AND
DIRECT SATELLITE BROADCASTING TO TECHNICAL
ASSISTANCE AND NATION-BUILDING IN THE "NEW"
COUNTRIES: AN ASIAN VIEWPOINT

by *K. Krishna Rao,* New Delhi*

> "Broadcasting via satellite offers an opportunity to the developing nations
> which have still not developed a general telecommunications network, for
> this new means permits the acceleration of their national programmes of
> integration, economic development, health, agriculture, education, communal
> development and culture ... direct broadcasting from satellites must be based
> on international cooperation to ensure its most effective utilization."[1]

The exploitation of the invention of telegraphy in the middle of the nineteenth century and the establishment of the International Telegraph
Union (now called the International Telecommunication Union) in 1865
led to the development of extensive international communication and
facilitated relations and cooperation between peoples across national
frontiers. The invention of radio telegraphy expanded further international activity in the field of telecommunication.

The rapidly developing technology in our times revolutionized the
whole field of international communication and brought about such developments as the transmission of voice and written messages, television
programs and data by satellites hovering thousands of miles above the
earth. Indeed, satellite communications, and especially the transmission
of television programs from them, constitute a "vital and almost mirac-
ulous link between countries and peoples" and pave the way towards
removing artificial barriers to communications among nations.[2] They
also present a special set of problems and point to the need for coope-
rations both in the operation of satellite systems and in their regulation.

There is an increasing interest both within and outside the United
Nations in the use of broadcasting satellites as a future communications
medium of tremendous potential importance. The full implications of this

---

* The views expressed herein are of the author personally, and not necessarily
of his government.
[1] Report of the Second Session, United Nations Working Group on Direct Broadcast Satellites, A/AC.105/66.
[2] Weil, *Communicating by Satellite: An International Discussion,* Carnegie Endowment for International Peace and The Twentieth Century Fund, New York, 1969.

113

new mass medium the spheres of technical assistance and nation-building, especially in the developing countries, are still a matter of both national and international studies. The United Nations Working Group on Direct Broadcast Satellites, UNESCO and ITU, among others, are already engaged in preparing comprehensive schemes of international cooperation in this field. Corresponding to the technological developments in this field, there is a need to make a beginning in the process of identifying the basic political, legal, cultural, economic and other problems involved here.

The Working Group on Direct Broadcast Satellites and Its Reports

By Resolution 2260 (XXII), the United Nations General Assembly requested the Committe on the Peaceful Uses of Outer Space "to study the technical feasibility of communication by direct broadcasts from satellites and the current and foreseeable developments in this field, as well as the implications of such developments." The Committee reported back to the General Assembly that widespread interest was aroused in the potential of direct broadcast satellites at the Seventh Session of its Legal Subcommittee and elsewhere because of the expected technical feasibility of such satellite systems. Taking these developments into account, the General Assembly approved, in Resolution 2453 (XXIII), "the establishment by the Committee on the Peaceful Uses of Outer Space of a Working Group to study and report on the technical feasibility of communications by direct broadcasts from satellites and the current and foreseeable developments in this field, including comparative user costs and other economic considerations, as well as the implications of such developments in the social, cultural, legal and other areas."

The first two reports of the Working Group[3] represent a substantial contribution to the fulfillment of the task set forth in the Resolution. At its First Session in February 1969, the Working Group considered the technical feasibility of communication by direct broadcast from satellites and gave the following estimated time scales of satellite broadcasting:

(i) Direct broadcast into *community* receivers could be close at hand. Technology currently under development might allow this in the mid-1970's.

(ii) Direct broadcast of television into *augmented* home receivers could become feasible technologically as soon as 1975.

(iii) Direct broadcasting television signals into existing, *unaugmented* home receivers on an operational basis is not foreseen for the period 1970-1985.

[3] U.N. Docs. A/AC.105/51 and A/AC.105/66, and Corr. 1 and 2.

114

At its Second Session in July and August 1969, the Working Group discussed the social, cultural, legal and other questions involved in direct broadcasts from satellites. It is obvious that direct broadcasts from satellites could be used for either domestic, regional or global services and that the problems that might arise regarding different patterns of service are not similar. It would appear that, in view of the small number of countries likely to establish domestic systems and the improbability of global systems, the most practical pattern of service will be the regional. The Working Group expressed the view that in the case of direct broadcasts from satellites for community television intended for purely domestic coverage, a government, while bound to fulfill its international legal obligation, will be able to adopt such regulations as it considers appropriate. However, limited problems of national spillover are envisaged at the stage of direct broadcasting into unaugmented home receivers for domestic coverage.

The cases of regional or global coverage appear to stand on a different footing inasmuch as they require regional or global cooperation and coordination in such matters as use of satellites, common technical standards, languages, time-sharing and program content. While a significant degree of control by individual governments appear possible in these cases, it is much more difficult in the case of direct broadcasting from satellites into unaugmented home receivers.

Benefits from direct broadcasts from satellites

The need to disseminate information to the masses is vital for the rapid and sustained growth of developing countries. Newspapers, movies, radio and television are the primary mass media. Of all these media, television constitutes an ideal medium to convey information and news to the broad masses of people—particularly to the illiterate segment of the population in rural areas in developing countries.

We need hardly draw attention here to the tremendous potentials of the peaceful utilization of direct broadcast satellites for the flow or exchange of information, intelligence and data in the interest of mankind. These have been indicated adequately in several national and international studies carried out so far by international organizations, such as the Food and Agriculture Organization, ITU and the World Meteorological Organization. The advent of cummunication satellites, however, has a special relevance to developing nations which have not still acquired an extensive infrastructure of telecommunication with older technologies.

Studies have revealed that broadcasting using satellites could be attractive when compared with conventional means of providing equivalent service, even though an optimum system in the future is expected to have ground telecommunications as well as satellite communications. There are unique opportunities for optimizing a system in respect of its cost and effectiveness where the existing investment is relatively small. India, for instance, can immensely profit from this situation provided it can use satellite communications for its national development meaningfully and with imagination. The UNESCO Study Group on Satellite Instructional Television has endorsed the unique contribution this new technology can make to developing nations and has identified India as a particularly appropriate area for early implementation.

Direct broadcasting from satellites into community receivers makes it possible to link together isolated rural communities and distant centers of population, and consequently it will have great practical benefits for educational, economic and social development. Studies that are being conducted in some developing countries like India, Indonesia and Brazil are a pointer in this regard. I may refer in this connection to a Memorandum of Understanding signed by the Department of Atomic Energy, India, and the National Aeronautics and Space Administration of the United States on September 18, 1969 to conduct jointly an instructional television experiment using the ATS-F satellite. The DAE-NASA experimental satellite TV project will lay emphasis on community viewing and on instructional TV as an aid to development in the fields of education, family planning, agriculture, social education and so on.

The DAE-NASA experiment is related to the following specific Indian instructional and technical objectives:

1. *Indian Instructional Objectives*
   a. *Primary Objectives*
   Contribute to family planning objectives
   Improve agricultural practices
   Contribute to national integration
   b. *Secondary Objectives*
   Contribute to general school and adult education
   Contribute to teacher training
   Improve health and hygiene

116

2. *Indian Technical Objectives*

Provide a system test of broadcast satellite TV for national development

Enhance capability in the design, manufacture, development, installation, operation, movement and maintenance of village TV receivers

Gain experience in the design, manufacture, installation, operation and maintenance of broadcast and/or distribution facilities to the extent that these are used in the experiment

Gain an opportunity to determine optimum receiver density, distribution, and scheduling techniques of audience attraction and organization and to solve problems involved in developing, preparing, presenting and transmitting TV program material

Broad Objectives of International Agreements

It is obvious that all uses of satellite communication require international cooperation which might best be reflected in international arrangements. On the basis of studies carried out by a number of international organizations and experts, UNESCO has stated that the broad objectives of these arrangements might include the following:

(i) ensuring the use of satellite communication in the public interest for peaceful purposes and for better understanding between nations; (ii) ensuring the availability of satellite communication to all States, irrespective of the stage of their social, economic and technical development, on a global and non-discriminatory basis; (iii) promoting organizational and administrative forms providing equitable access to communication satellite systems, with special regard to smaller countries and developing areas: (iv) providing proper access to global and regional communication satellite systems by the United Nations and the specialized agencies; (v) ensuring equitable use of the radio frequency spectrum; (vi) promoting harmonious integration of satellite communication facilities into present and planned telecommunication networks used for mass media purposes; (vii) promoting favourable conditions for institutional or professional agreements enabling mass media to increase the exchange of news programmes and programme materials; (viii) encouraging the use of satellite communication by different users, with special regard to the development of broadcasting and the flow of educational, scientific, cultural and information materials.[4]

Legal aspects

The legal aspects of satellite broadcasting were examined at the Second Session of the Working Group in some depth. There seems to be

[4] A/AC.105/60.

universal agreement in the group that among the international legal instruments already applicable to direct broadcasts from satellites are the U.N. Charter, the Treaty on Principles Governing the Activities of States in the Exploration and Use of Outer Space, Including the Moon and Other Celestial Bodies, and the relevant articles of the ITU Convention and Radio Regulations. Attention has also been drawn in this connection to a number of relevant principles contained in the General Assembly resolutions relating to peaceful uses of outer space.

Among the Charter principles applicable in this context are those concerning the sovereign equality of states, the development of friendly relations, the achievement of international cooperation, promotion of respect for human rights and fundamental freedoms, and the principle of non-interference in matters within the domestic jurisdiction of any state.

It may also be pointed out in this connection that the Draft Declaration on Principles of International Law Concerning Friendly Relations and Cooperation among States in Accordance with the Charter of the United Nations, as contained in the report of the 1970 United Nations Special Committee on Friendly Relations, also contains appropriate provisions which should be taken into account in this connection. In its preambular part, the Draft recites as follows:

> "Noting that the great political, economic and social changes and scientific progress which have taken place in the world since the adoption of the Charter of the United Nations give increased importance to these principles and to the need *for their more effective application in the conduct of states wherever carried on.*"

The duty of states to cooperate with one another is, of course, itself one of the fundamental principles of international law, and the Draft Declaration continues in this vein:

> "States have the duty to co-operate with one another, irrespective of the differences in their political, economic and social systems, in the various spheres of international relations, in order to maintain international peace and security and to promote international economic stability and progress, the general welfare of nations and international co-operation free from discrimination based on such differences. . ."

The working Group has also drawn attention to Articles 3 and 6 of the Outer Space Treaty. Article 3 provides:

> "States Parties to the Treaty shall carry on activities in the exploration and use of Outer Space, including the moon and other celestial bodies, in accordance with International law, including the Charter of the United Nations, in the interest of maintaining international peace and security and promoting international cooperation and understanding."

118

Article 6 of the same Treaty provides that states shall bear international responsibility for national activities in outer space, whether they are undertaken by states, international organizations or non-governmental entities.

Among other principles relevant in this connection are the universally accepted principles concerning the common interest of all mankind in the exploration and use of outer space for peaceful purposes and for the benefit and in the interests of all countries, irrespective of their degree of economic or scientific development.

The Working Group also discussed questions concerning the protection of copyright and neighboring rights and the need for an internationally acceptable instrument protecting television programs transmitted or broadcast via satellites against retransmission and public utilization of such programs without the authorization of the originating television organization. It expressed the view that the questions should receive urgent study by concerned international bodies like UNESCO and the BIRPI. The question of spillover of television broadcasts into neighboring countries also needs careful examination, and a solution to this problem should seek to avoid giving offense to the states affected by it.

Content of broadcast

The rules concerning program content of satellite broadcasts have been the subject of discussion both within the United Nations and in other international bodies. Though no concrete agreement seems to have emerged from these deliberations, the general legal issues have already been indicated. A meeting of experts on the use of space communication by the mass media held at UNESCO in 1965 drew attention to "the possibility that a satellite programme service might easily cross national boundaries and be receivable where it was not wanted, the possible use of satellites for propaganda, and potential differences of opinion about the content of international programme service." The meeting concluded that these problems "point to the need for careful planning and cooperation, both nationally and internationally."

Rules and principles with regard to program content should be based on "state sovereignty." No state or a group a of states could broadcast programs to other states without the approval of the latter through bilateral or multilateral agreements. This principle flows from the well-established rules of general international law relating to national sovereignty and non-interference in the internal affairs of states.

Broadly speaking, states are bound by the relevant principles of international law and the Charter of the United Nations in satellite broadcasts as in any other field.

Generally speaking, the content of broadcasts may relate to either political, cultural and social or commercial aspects. The political aspects of content of broadcasts are of major significance in view of the likely impact on an international scale, and particularly on developing nations which might find themselves at the mercy of major powers transmitting propaganda and other offensive programs. Regulations in this regard should take due account of principles concerning the prohibition of interference in the internal affairs of states, incitement by war or violation of human rights and freedoms and war propaganda. It is essential that direct satellite broadcasting should not become an instrument of harmful propaganda and the fanning of hatred and intolerance among states. As stated in the Outer Space Treaty, the U.N. General Assembly resolution 110(II) of November 3, 1947, which condemned propaganda designed or likely to provoke or encourage any threat to the peace, breach of the peace or act of aggression is also applicable to outer space.

A suggestion has been made in this connection for the establishment of a code of conduct or program standards through international cooperation. However, doubts have been expressed as to the feasibility of establishing a detailed code. It is nevertheless essential that this aspect of the matter should be further studied with a view to seeking protection against unwanted political interference.

Conclusion

Like all other space activities, direct broadcast satellites require international cooperation and international arrangements inasmuch as they do not have at present a comprehensive legal system regulating them. The common interest of mankind in this new area demands common action. Unless this is done, situations involving conflicting claims, interference, jamming and international discord might ensue.

As the General Assembly of the United Nations has stated in its Resolution 1721 D(XVI) of December 20, 1961 and 2601 A(XXIV) of December 16, 1969, communications by means of satellites should be available to the nations of the world as soon as practicable on a global and non-discriminatory basis, and states parties to negotiations regarding international arrangements in the field of satellite communication should constantly bear this principle in mind so that its ultimate realization will not be impaired.

The development of communications by means of satellites would offer immense assistance to developing countries in the fight against illiteracy, and help disseminate information concerning agriculture, health and family planning and community developent. To use this new technology effectively as a means of promoting national integration and development, experience needs to be gained in regard to content and programming. It is, therefore, obvious that developing countries need assistance to take full advantage of this mass medium, not only from industrially advanced nations but also from international organizations such as FAO, the World Health Organization, WMO, UNESCO, the International Labor Organization and the United Nations Development Program.

Taking due account of the relevant principles of the Charter of the United Nations, the growing space law and the ITU Convention and Radio Regulations, it would appear that the most basic and important principles of international law relating to direct broadcasting would be those concerning sovereignty and state responsibility, non-intervention in the internal affairs of another state and the common interest of all mankind in outer space and in international cooperation in the exploration and use of outer space for peaceful purposes only and for the benefit and in the interests of all countries, irrespective of their degree of economic or scientific development.

Chapter 9

THE CONTRIBUTION OF TELECOMMUNICATIONS AND
DIRECT SATELLITE BROADCASTING TO TECHNICAL
ASSISTANCE AND NATION-BUILDING IN THE "NEW"
COUNTRIES: AN AFRICAN VIEWPOINT

by *T. O. Elias,* Lagos

I

In the middle of 1961, the United Kingdom Government, on behalf of
the partner governments, issued simultaneous invitations to the Federation of Nigeria, Ghana and the Federation of Malaya to become parties to the Commonwealth Telegraphs Agreement of 1948 and a member of the Commonwealth Telecommunications Board.

The Imperial Wireless and Cable Conference of 1928 had decided
to amalgamate in one company the existing assets and services of all
the Commonwealth overseas telegraph system. The following year Imperial and International Communications Ltd. was formed, and in 1934
it was renamed Cable and Wireless Ltd. on the terms that (a) the ap-
pointment of the chairman and one other director was subject to the
approval of the British Government, (b) the Company should consult an
Imperial Communications Advisory Committee on all policy matters,
(c) the Company should comply with the directions of Commonwealth
governments to safeguard strategic requirements and (d) the British
Government might ensure control of the system in an emergency.

The Eastern and Associated Telegraph Companies already had a
world-wide cable system which the new company took over in addition
to the beam wireless services and Atlantic cables of the British Post
Office, the Pacific Cable Board cables between Canada and Australia,
the Marconi wireless telegraph services in the United Kingdom and
financial interests in wireless telegraph companies in India, South Africa, Canada, Australia, Spain Portugal, Austria, Switzerland, Egypt,
Argentina, Brazil and Chile. Between 1929 and 1939, the work of integrating the cable and the wireless systems and services made great progress, and a solid foundation was laid for the radiotelephone network.

As a result of experience during the Second World War, Australia
voiced misgivings about the constitution of the Commonwealth over-

122

seas telecommunications system. The ensuing Commonwealth Telecommunications Conference, held in London in 1945, recommended fundamental changes in the Commonwealth telecommunications services, public ownership of these services by all Commonwealth governments, replacement of the Commonwealth Communications Council by a new board with wider functions on which all the governments in the Commonwealth would be represented and financial contributions by Commonwealth members for the maintenance and use of the cable system.

On May 11, 1948, the governments of the United Kingdom, Canada, Australia, New Zealand, South Africa, India and Southern Rhodesia (all being referred to as "the partner governments") signed the Commonwealth Telegraphs Agreement under which they undertook to carry out the recommendations of the 1945 conference. Thus was established the Commonwealth Telecommunications Board, which was duly incorporated by the (U.K.) Commonwealth Telecommunications Act of 1949. Ceylon became a partner government and a board member in June 1951; Southern Rhodesia was replaced in July 1954 by the Federation of Rhodesia and Nyasaland, which itself ceased to exist in 1961; and South Africa, by withdrawing from the Commonwealth, ceased to be a partner government and a board member in 1961 in accordance with Clause 10 (1) of the Agreement. Under Clauses 1 and 2, the United Kingdom Government directed the British Post Office to take over effective April 1, 1950 the assets and services of Cable and Wireless Ltd. in the United Kingdom; New Zealand and Ceylon similarly nominated their post offices as their national bodies in 1951; Canada and Australia each established a public corporation as her national body, while India nominated a body called the Government of India Overseas Communications Service. The board consists of a chairman appointed by the partner governments, one representative of each of them, and one representative appointed by the United Kingdom to represent Commonwealth territories that are not directly represented by other members. Pakistan was for a while represented by an observer. Nigeria, Ghana and Malaya maintained contact with the board through the Commonwealth Relations Office, which regularly supplied them with the board's memoranda and minutes untill the 1961 invitation.

The board's principal functions may be summarized as follows:

1. To make recommendations to the partner governments and to national bodies on the following matters relating to their external telecommunications system:

a. The formulation and execution of the joint telecommunications policy of the partner governments, including the fixing of rates.

b. Coordination of the development of the cable and wireless systems of the British Commonwealth.

c. Extensions to and alterations of the telecommunications systems of the British Commonwealth.

d. The provision and, where appropriate, the apportionment among national bodies of capital expenditure on projects.

e. Coordination with the appropriate authorities on telecommunication matters affecting the defense of the British Commonwealth or any part thereof.

f. Coordination of research in telecommunication matters conducted by national bodies.

g. The exchange of personnel between the board and national bodies.

h. Any other telecommunication matter which may be referred to the board by any of the partner governments or any national body.

2. At the request of the partner governments or national bodies, to conduct negotiations with foreign telecommunication interests on their behalf.

3. To promote and research in telecommunications matters.

4. To set up and administer a central fund for the receipt of the net revenues of the national bodies.

There can be not doubt about the advantages of such services to the "new" countries, since efficient and inexpensive telecommunication services are vital to their well-being and to the furtherance of Commonwealth and world trade. The board provides the machinery by which the pooling and coordination of the external telecommunications of the Commonwealth countries could be efficiently and cheaply effected. The system thus evolved is widely known as the common user system. The board directs, advises and exercises control over the running expenses of the system but does not perform any operational functions, nor does it provide capital for development. The national bodies of the member countries as well as the nationalized company of Cable and Wireless Ltd. together provide the needed capital for both operation and development. Cable and Wireless Ltd. is thus an agent of the board for maintaining the cable links between the national bodies of the various Commonwealth countries, and it finances development (in certain sections of the overall system that is of interest to it) out of the profits it makes by operating its services in various parts of the world. Through its central fund, the board provides the machinery for apportioning the cost of operating and maintaining the international links of the common user system between the users of the system under a "wayleave scheme."

The conditions of admission of new Commonwealth countries are laid down in Clause 9 of the 1948 agreement as follows: "The Partner Governments may admit the Government of any other part of the British Commonwealth and Empire as a party to this Agreement on such terms (including the acquisition of shares in local Companies and of local assets) as may be agreed and as from such date as may be agreed, the Government so admitted shall become a Partner Government for the purposes of this Agreement and the provisions of this Agreement may on the recommendation of the Board be modified in such manner as may be necessary or expedient to adapt them to the terms and consequences of the admission and as so modified shall be binding on the Partner Governments including the Government so admitted." The partner governments had, however, agreed that new members need not be under any obligation to acquire the local assets of the companies that operated their external telecommunications, as was required by Clause 1 of the Agreement, unless they themselves chose to do so. The new members were not required to sign the 1948 Agreement; it was sufficient if they submitted written acceptances of the invitation. It became necessary for both new and old members to sign the draft Supplementary Agreement, an obligation which is implied by an acceptance of the invitation. The older members could not operate their own services independently, and the newer would fare even worse were they to try to do so. The more economic operation of the system provided an opportunity for the national bodies either to make larger profits or to reduce the cable rates between points in the system. The partner governments have, quite rightly, chosen the latter alternative. The board has long recognized that rapid advances in telecommunication techniques, such as round-the-world submarine telephone cables and communications via satellites, require maximum collaboration if the full benefits are to be realized. Participation by the new states in this enterprise would greatly assist them in the development of both their internal and their external telecommunications system. Of course, new members must contribute annually to the board's central fund and must consult the board on matters affecting the common user system; and no member can withdraw for a period of eight years.

Nigeria, Ghana, Malaya and, since 1961, most of the countries in Africa and Asia that have attained independence have accepted the in-

125

vitation and become parties to the 1948 Agreement and members of the board. Ghana, for instance, has established a public corporation as its national body while Nigeria has nominated Nigerian External Telecommunications Ltd., of which the Federal Government owns 51 per cent of the shares and Cable and Wireless Ltd. the remainder, as its national body. The Government of Singapore has established a statutory corporation entitles the Singapore Telecommunications Board in which the Government and Cable and Wireless hold 51 per cent and 49 per cent of the shares respectively. (Ghana declared in 1962 that she would assume responsibility for all her external communications through the Ghana Posts and Telecommunications Administration.) It will thus be seen that practice varies as to the manner of meeting the requirements of the 1948 Agreement and of the board. All the new states have their nominees on the board.

Nigerian External Telecommunications Ltd. now maintains direct radio links with some nineteen world capitals through which it provides constant telephone, telegraph and telex services to all parts of the world from its well-equipped receiving station at Ikoyi and its modern and equally well-equipped transmitter station at Ikorodu. The Company operates, for firms and local representatives of overseas companies, the highest number of leased overseas telegraph channels from any Commonwealth country. Telex services are also available directly to Europe via the United Kingdom and the United States and to some African countries like Dahomey, Sierra Leone, Liberia, the Ivory Coast, Cameroun, Ghana and the Congo (Kinshasa). Also provided are other services like press reception, facsimile transmission and reception and transmission of voicecasts. The great emphasis placed on staff training has resulted in Nigerians occupying all management posts from the general manager downwards, and particularly all technical posts at the lower levels. There has been a corresponding decrease in the number of expatriate staff from twenty-four to four without loss in efficiency and profitability.

II

In 1960, the U.S. National Aeronautics and Space Administration (NASA) proposed to establish a group of tracking stations in Africa as part of its communications network. The group was made up of Kano in Northern Nigeria, Zanzibar, and Tananarive in Madagascar. The

126

three stations were planned so as to be able to cummunicate with one another, with space capsules in orbit and directly with the NASA Space Flight Center in Greenbelt, Maryland.

An agreement was necessary, however, between the United States and the other governments regarding permission to build the stations. In the case of Nigeria, the agreement enabled NASA to set up two complementary stations in Kano: a transmitter with facilities for telephone, teletype and telemetry transmission, built near the Nigerian Government's Civil Aviation Station at Kofar Naisa in Kano; and a receiving station for the same services at the Daura Airstrip twenty-seven miles north of the Kofar Naisa station.

It is interesting to note that NASA used the Kano Tracking Station for the Mercury and the Gemini programs and that this station was the first to be in direct communication with John Glenn, the first American astronaut to orbit the earth.

The operational staff at the Kano station between 1960 and the end of 1962 consisted of a number of Americans especially recruited by NASA and also staff at first wholly provided by Cable and Wireless Ltd., London. But between 1962 and December 1966 the operational staff consisted of Americans and the Nigerian staff assigned to the station by Nigerian External Telecommunications Ltd. Needless to say, quite apart from the interesting results of the space enterprise, Nigeria was able to gain a good deal of scientific experience for its personnel in this field of telecommunications.

When the satellite communications system became sufficiently developed in the last three years, NASA recognized its greater reliability and decided to close down in December 1966 the Kano station, which relied mainly on high-frequency radio communication. Some of the most important telecommunications equipments were removed, but NASA presented Nigeria with quite a large quantity of equipment. The Nigerian Civil Aviation Department has since taken over all the items left behind by NASA.

Also of real interest is the fact that the federal government of Nigeria had already spent over £ 100,000 for the purchase and installation of telecommunications equipment in pursuance and implementation of the World Weather Watch at Kano Telecommunications Center. The regional Meteorological Training Center, Ikeja, Nigeria, is one of the international centers in Africa. Under a special agreement, the World Meteorological Organization will continue to supply equipment and technical, advisory, operational and training experts to the Kano Telecommunications Center. It is also expected that facilities will be provided for a central forecasting and analysis center.

III

The recent development of satellite earth stations is an event of great significance to the entire world. These stations are concerned mainly with the routing of external traffic, terminal as well as transit. As they are potentially acquisitions of great security value, it is now the practice of many countries to entrust the management of their earth stations to the national bodies that are responsible for their external telecommunications services.

Early in 1965, the Government of the United States proposed to the Government of Nigeria the signing of two agreements for the establishment of a global commercial communications satellite system. It may be recalled that in 1963 Nigeria participated with the United States in this field by becoming the only tracking station in Africa for the Syncom project, which resulted in the successful launching into orbit of the satellite Telstar. This satellite made it possible, in August 1963, for the late Prime Minister of Nigeria, Sir Abubakar Tafawa Balewa, to speak to the late President John F. Kennedy of the United States. Through U.S. initiative, arrangements were then put in hand for the establishment of a universal organization for the exploitation of satellite communications on a global scale.

One of the agreements established interim arrangements for a global commercial communications satellite system, while the other set forth procedures, rights and duties during the proposed interim arrangements for the satellite system. The two agreements entered into force on August 20, 1964.

The Agreement Establishing Interim Arrangements for a Global Commercial Communication Satellite System establishes the principle that a single commercial system should be immediately established and expanded to provide world coverage on a non-discriminatory basis. Each government signatory to the agreement designates a communications entity, either governmental or private, to be its participant. The United States' participant is the Communications Satellite Corporation. The agreement provides that each participating government's entity will contribute a certain percentage of the capital funds required for the space segment of the system. As new countries join it, the owner-

128

ship percentage of the participants will be reduced *pro rata*. Each country or group of countries with a percentage of 1.5 or more is entitled to have a representative on the Interim Communication Satellite Committee, which has overall responsibility for the operation and development of the system. There is a further provision that, for a period of six months from August 20, 1964, any member of the International Telecommunication Union might adhere to the agreement on the same terms as the initial signatories. The Committee determines the allocation of investment percentage for every new participant. It also approves access of ground stations to the space segment and is charged with allocating satellite communication channels both to the co-owners and to the authorized communication entities of other countries that might wish to have access to the system through a ground station on their territory but who did not wish to contribute to the capital cost of the space segment. Such access would be on an equitable and non-discriminatory basis. After the expiration of the first six months, other nations might still accede to the agreement on terms to be determined by the Committee, having regard to the fact that the original participants should be equitably compensated for the risks they incurred in establishing the system.

The Special Agreement on Arbitration, signed by the national entities, describes the relationship between the Committee and the U.S. Communications Satellite Corporation, which acts as the manager of the system. It covers the functions and procedures of the Committee, operational policies, procurement for the system and financial arrangements, including rates and charges. The Agreement is co-terminous with the Inter-Government Agreement, which provided that by January 1, 1969 the Committee should render a report to each party containing its recommendation concerning the definitive arrangements for the international global system which should supersede the Interim Arrangements. The report of the Committee was to be considered at an international conference to be convened by the United States within three months of the submission of the report.

Since a communication satellite which is practical for commercial purposes has a receiver to pick up radio signals from a transmitter on the earth's surface and an amplifier and an transmitter to repeat the amplified signals, which are then received at another point on the earth's surface through a highly sensitive receiver, it is capable of broad-band transmission useful for all types of electronics communication including voice, telegraphy, high-speed data, fascimile and television. There are

129

at present two types of this satellite: the medium altitude satellite like the Telstar and Relay, and the high-altitude or synchronous satellite, like the Syncom 3, launched on August 18, 1964, in order to achieve a truly stationary orbit. Although a communication satellite "system" has yet to be achieved, it has great potential for providing much-needed circuits to areas that are not now served by high-quality communications, such as Africa, Asia and Latin America. The United States initiated and sponsored Resolution 1721 of December 1961 in which the General Assembly of the United Nations unanimously expressed its belief "that communication by means of satellites should be available to the nations of the world as soon as practicable on a global and non-discriminatory basis." The United States Communications Satellite Act of 1962 embodies the policy of establishing, in cooperation with other countries, the commercial system that will serve the communication needs of the United States and other countries and that will contribute to world peace and understanding. It is expected that the new and expanded telecommunication system will be employed to provide services to economically less developed countries and areas no less than the more highly developed ones.

As satellite communication is considered the best means of long-distance communication compared with submarine cables and high-frequency communications, it affords a good deal of flexibility in carrying international traffic to the main switching centers, from which by automatic routing a network can be established in a relatively short time. This is a new development which is of considerable importance, especially to the new states.

Under the agreement setting up the international organization, countries wishing to become co-owners by contributing 1.5 percent are expected to provide and operate a ground station which may be equipped to provide transmission and reception for television and telegraph circuits. The Hughes Aircraft Company and Nippon Electric Company Ltd., which have commercial interests in the production of ground station equipment, might be in a position to arrange loans for countries. Each user country is also required to pay for leasing the satellite channel. Any country that first becomes a user of the system by possessing a ground station in Africa might become a switching center for all other countries in the African region, or at least over a wide area of it. Such a government might also have a say in matters such as channel allocation, tariffs and so on. A real possibility, insofar as Africa is concerned, is that a number of friendly countries could jointly become co-owners

130

within the framework of the Organization of African Unity's Communications and Transport Commission.

Before such a joint enterprise becomes feasible, however, individual countries have had to arrange for their own earth stations. It has been recorded that, as at September 30, 1969, no less than thirty-two earth stations were already in operation in twenty-five countries, and the figure is expected to reach fifty by the end of 1970. This phenomenal growth is a real indication that most countries appreciate the advantages to be derived from participation in the development of satellite communication. The vista of hope and success symbolized by this initial global system will be considerably enhanced by the launching toward the end of 1970 of the Intelsat IV series of satellites.

Despite the high cost of participation, it is gratifying to note that an increasing number of "new" countries are already participating, either from their own national resources or with the assistance of loans and grants from outside sources. In Africa, Morocco has now completed her own earth station, and Kenya will soon complete hers, these countries having been greatly assisted by outside finance. Nigeria was the first country in Africa to accede in 1965 to the global Communications Satellite System (Comsat) by signing the two agreements already discussed above. Telcom, Inc. of Virginia was appointed engineering consultants under a contract which required that they should be responsible to the Nigerian Government for the selection of a suitable site for the station, the preparation of specifications for the electronic equipment and of bid documents, evaluation of tenders and inspection and surveillance of the project implementation. Nigeria has almost completed her own earth station at Lanlate with funds provided entirely by its Posts and Telecommunications Department. The contract for the 300-line International Telephone Switching Center was awarded to the Bell Telephone Manufacturing Company as the result of a competitive tender on the condition that satisfactory payment terms should be made with the Nigerian Government. Similarly, the contract for the Nigerian Communications Satellite Earth Station project was awarded to the General Telephone and Electronics International, Inc., subject also to agreement on satisfactory payment terms. This company has previously built complete earth stations for Thailand, Chile and the Philippines as well as the U.S.

When fully operational, the earth station will be in the charge of Nigerian External Telecommunications Ltd. on an agency basis. Since this company is under the control of the Nigerian Government, it will

131

not be difficult to ensure that the right national policies are followed in such matters as security, pooling of resources with other African countries or discharging her responsibilities as a possible international switching center. The center is the gateway where all circuits coming from or going to the earth station terminate. This gateway is then connected to the inland telephone system, thus providing facilities for international telephone, telex and telegraph services. It constitutes the link between the internal communications system and the earth station.

IV

In 1959, the International Telecommunication Union held a Plenipotentiary Conference in Geneva at which it was decided to establish a World Plan Committee and a number of Regional Plan Committees to be jointly approved by the Plenary Assemblies of ITU's International Consultative Committees. It was intended that the Regional Plan Committees would be responsible for developing a general plan for the international telecommunication network. They were to refer to the International Consultative Committees questions that were of particular interest to new or developing countries and that came within the Consultative Committees' terms of reference. The Plan Committee for Africa was accordingly established, and its first meeting, held in Dakar, Senegal, in 1962, was attended by all the telecommunication administrations in Africa.

It should be noted that in 1962 there were only a few direct communications channels between African countries and that these were only by high-frequency radio. Some of these services were chiefly on a schedule basis. The Committee examined in some detail the existing telecommunications network in Africa and made a number of recommendations for their improvement. The meeting agreed to submit a series of reports to the next meeting of the World Plan Committee, scheduled to take place in Rome in November 1963. At the latter meeting, the Regional Plan Committees for Latin America, Asia and Africa were present.

The representatives of African countries took this opportunity to review their Dakar recommendations and to consider a number of proposals from member countries. For instance, Nigeria put forward proposals for the establishment of direct telecommunications services with a number of African countries and, in consequence of the agreement

132

at the Rome Conference, Nigerian External Telecommunications Ltd. established, between 1964 and 1966, direct communications by telephone and telegraph and in some cases by telex with the following African countries—the Congo (Kinshasa), the Congo (Brazzaville), Cameroun, Dahomey, Ethiopia, Equatorial Guinea, Gambia, Guinea, the Ivory Coast, East Africa (including Kenya, Tanzania and Uganda), Niger, Liberia, Senegal, Sierra Leone and the Sudan.

The services between Nigeria and these countries have been maintained and, indeed, improved from time to time to ensure efficient service on a schedule basis. Three more African countries have since been added to the list.

Apart from such bilateral arrangements, there has always been a need for multilateral agreements linking a group of countries. It was in order to be in a position to attract technical assistance from more developed countries that the Economic Commission for Africa and the International Telecommunication Union jointly established a mission at the ECA headquarters in Addis Ababa, Ethiopia. The arrangement is that ITU recruits telecommunications experts whom it posts to the ECA headquarters to carry out two principal functions—coordinate work on the establishment of a Pan-African telecommunications network and provide technical advice to African countries. The ECA/ITU mission also gives advice when matters affecting the Transport and Telecommunication Commission of the Organization of African Unity (also based in Addis Ababa) are referred to the ECA headquarters.

At the second meeting of the Regional Plan Committee for Africa, held in January 1967 in Addis Ababa, Ethiopia, a further and more intensified review of the various developments in the field of Pan-African telecommunications was made. One of the more important decisions was that more sophisticated systems such as coaxial cables, microwave and satellite systems should be introduced in place of the high-frequency radio system. An agreement was also reached that Nigeria should play host to the next CCITT Regional Plan Committee meeting scheduled for January 18-29, 1971.

As a result of the Addis Ababa meeting's recommendations, the United Nations Special Fund called upon ITU to provide experts to conduct a survey of the Pan-African telecommunication network. The Special Fund offered to finance the project. Two teams of experts, one for West Africa and the other for East Africa, were duly commissioned, and the survey was completed in November 1969. The reports are still being awaited at the time of writing. It is expected that, if the recommendations are acceptable to the African countries, loans to finance the various projects will be sought from the African Development Bank.

In the meantime, a number of African countries have, as we have seen, embarked on the construction of satellite earth stations which will provide Intra-African and intercontinental telecommunication facilities. Morocco completed her own in September 1970; the East African Community (based in Kenya) was to be in operation by May 1970; Nigeria will complete her own station before the end of 1970. Other countries expected to construct satellite earth stations by 1972 are Senegal, the Ivory Coast, Cameroun, Zambia, the Sudan and Ethiopia. About that same year, Nigeria, Morocco, the Sudan and Ethiopia should be able to communicate via an Atlantic Ocean satellite. Similarly, by 1972, when the second antenna for the Nigerian earth station is expected to be in operation, East Africa, Zambia and Nigeria might be able to communicate via an Indian Ocean satellite.

It will be noticed that the development of a Pan-African telecommunication network has been rather slow. This has been caused by the continuing interest of some of the colonial powers in the external telecommunications services of the newly independent states in Africa, particularly in all the Francophone countries in which the French-controlled company, France Cables et Radio, still holds an exclusive franchise. So rigidly has the pattern of telecommunications in Africa been set by the former colonial powers that it is still easier in many cases for the capital of an African country to communicate with the capital of the relevant colonial power than it is to communicate between contiguous African countries unless they were previously under the same power.

Given the current efforts of the International Telecommunication Union, the Economic Commission for Africa and the Organization of African Unity and the financial assistance of the African Development Bank, there is every reason to believe that African countries will before long be able to communicate directly with one another in almost the same way as European countries do.

The development of telecommunications in both Latin America and Asia is likely to be of equal significance in the next few months. The countries of these developing areas have, as we have seen, been building satellite earth stations, and the results are already accelerating the economic and social advance of the people.

In all the three developing areas, international finance has played and will continue to play a useful role in the contribution which satellite

134

communications is making toward their commercial and technological progress in the second half of the century.

V

One of the products of the developing satellite technology is broadcasting by satellite, which raises a number of technical, economic and legal problems beyond those we have seen so far in the case of radio broadcasts received by one country from others. Although the original forecast by the United Nations Working Group on Direct Broadcast Satellites was that by 1975 it would be feasible to have broadcasting put into community receivers for redistribution to home sets, the group has now predicted that 1972, or 1973, when the United States is expected to launch the Indian Ocean satellite, is a more realistic date.

According to the discussion at the International Conference held in September 1969 in Talloires, France, under the joint auspices of the Carnegie Endowment for International Peace and the Twentieth Century Fund, New York, direct broadcasting in one form or another is expected to become a reality in the 1970's in India, Pakistan, Indonesia and Latin America (especially Brazil). It seems very likely that Nigeria, Morocco and East Africa (Kenya) will also have it during the same decade. While direct satellite broadcasting is of great importance to the "new" nations, it must not be thought that the "older" ones will not benefit from it. Indeed, it has been suggested that the United States, Europe and Canada might also find direct broadcasting useful.

Some of the major problems attendant upon satellite broadcasting are its high cost, the clear possibility that it will interfere with terrestial programming and the need for nations using it to accept responsibility for any harmful effects that its use may have on other nations. The U.N. Working Group has also pointed out the need for legal constraint on user nations against broadcasting unwanted programs into other countries and to control programs in the hands of the broadcasters themselves. With regard to the problem of limiting unwanted spillover of broadcasts, whether intentional or unintentional, a suggestion has been made that world-wide broadcasts will not be common but that regional and domestic programs will be the ideal, in which case the greater degree of homogeneity among neighboring states should reduce areas of friction due to offensive or propaganda programs. Another suggestion is that an international code similar to the body of rules of internation-

135

al air law is the answer. In this regard, the two launching nations—the United States and the Soviet Union—have been asked to deny the use of their facilities to any country using them for broadcasting objectionable material.

As regards placing program control in the hands of broadcasters themselves as a means of preventing offensive broadcasts, it seems too early in the development of satellite broadcasting to ask these technicians to formulate a fixed set of rules. It has been said that, in order to minimize the chances of possible governmental intervention, some non-official agencies like foundations or universities might be requested to draw up proposals for broadcaster cooperation in determining program content. In this connection, broadcasters in neighboring countries have, in the European Broadcasting Union's Eurovision, reached agreement on acceptable broadcasts for distribution over a wide area. Other similar institutions are the International Radio and Television Organization, the Asian Broadcasting Union, and the Union of National Radio and Television Organizations of Africa—all of which should be strengthened to promote cooperation among broadcasters in their respective areas. The legal, technical and economic problems posed by direct satellite broadcasting, especially in the "new" states, should first be tackled in the existing and in new regional institutions as a step toward the ultimate achievement of an international consensus.

As an associate member of the European Broadcasting Union, the Nigerian Broadcasting Corporation is entitled to attend the Union's general meetings and professional committees and to obtain all the information it collects and disseminates. Besides participating in discussions at the United Nations and at UNESCO, the Union has promoted studies of the legal and financial aspects of satellite broadcasting. The Nigerian Broadcasting Corporation is also a full and active member of the Union of National Radio and Television Organizations of Africa (URTNA) which, although it has not done much work in satellite broadcasting, has nevertheless regularly sent observers to U.N. and UNESCO meetings on the subject as well as taking an active interest in all the past and current studies. This Union promises to go into satellite broadcasting in earnest before long. Yet another body of considerable interest to developing countries and of which both the Director-General and the Director of Programs of the Nigerian Broadcasting Corporation are members is the International Broadcast Institute, the membership of which consists only of individuals in their own right. It is not a broadcasting organization, nor does it represent any group of organizations;

136

it is a body of professional communicators interested in the development of broadcasting and anxious to initiate studies of the new technology and its implications for communication. Financed by American and European foundations, the Institute is currently promoting two studies on satellite broadcasting: the first is a "tariff" study analyzing the present costs of satellite broadcasting facilities and suggesting ways in which the tariff can be brought within the reach of even the "new" nations; the second is a legal study intended to provide information on copyright and other legal aspects of satellite broadcasting. The results of both studies are expected to be published sometime in 1971.

We have already referred to the negotiations and meetings which have been taking place since February 1969 for the internationalization of Intelsat. Let us hope that this objective will be realized at the meeting scheduled to take place in Washington, D.C. in November 1970. If agreement can be reached at this meeting, it will be a useful addition to the developing international law of communication.

Chapter 10

SOUTH AMERICAN CONTRIBUTIONS TO SOLUTION OF THE
JURIDICAL PROBLEMS OF TELECOMMUNICATIONS AND
DIRECT SATELLITE BROADCASTING

by *Haroldo Valladao,* Rio de Janeiro

The origins of the international law of communications go back over a
century. The early international conventions forming the basis of this
law begin with the International Telegraph Convention of 1865.

The history of this activity at the general, international level has parallels in the history of various regional activities, including those of the
Americas.

In Latin America the first such regional activity was the 1924 Inter-
American Electrical Communication Conference held in Mexico. It
was followed by the Inter-American Radio Agreements and the Inter-
American Radio Conferences: Havana in 1937, Santiago in 1940, Rio
de Janeiro in 1945 and Washington in 1949.

Latin Americans have made additional regional arrangements in the
South American Regional Agreements on Radiocommunication: Buenos Aires, 1935 and Rio de Janeiro, 1937 (later revised).

Juridically, the law of communications has been considered under
the general heading of international law and the specific heading of
international administrative law. The works of Verdross and Bustaman-
te discuss the purposes, powers and natures of various international
unions created since the nineteenth century, including the International
Telecommunication Union, established in 1865, and the International
Postal Union, established in 1874.

Before World War II, a new notion became dominant among the
scholars treating administrative matters which concerned, in one way
or another, the international community. According to this new notion,
communications belonged in the category of international public service, rather than that of mere public service, and was thus transferred
out of the sphere of domestic or internal administrative law into that
of international administrative law. Consequently, such international
bodies as the Telecommunication and Postal Unions, which are open
to the participation of all states and even to protectorates and colonies,
and possibly even to non-governmental enterprises, became international associations of a non-political character.

Some juridical principles of telegraphic services which were established in the 1865 Paris Conference are well worth noting. The states agreed upon two parallel frameworks in the field of telecommunications —one, a Convention and the other Radio Regulations. This dual system proved efficient and permitted periodic revision through International Conferences. The Berlin and London Radiotelegraph Conferences and later the Conferences on Telecommunications, utilized this approach. At the last Telecommunications Conference in Montreux, held in 1965, representatives of private enterprises—duly authorized by the Contracting States—were allowed to be present.

The basic juridical principle of telecommunication—that of utilization of the services by all—originated in the Telegraph Convention of 1865, Article 4 of which states that the High Contracting Parties recognize the rights of all people to correspond by means of international telegraph. (*"Les H.P.C. reconnaissent à toutes personnes le droit de correspondre au moyen des télégraphes internationaux."*) This idea was repeated in the Saint Petersburg Convention (Article 1), the London Radiotelegraph Convention (Article 17) and the Telecommunication Convention of Montreux (Article 31), which states: "The Members and the associated Members concede to the public the right to exchange correspondence. The services, the fees and the grantings shall be the same for all users, in each category of correspondence, without any priority or preference."

The basic limitation on that right first appeared in the 1865 Convention (Article 19); it was repeated at the Saint Petersburg Convention of 1874 (Article 7) and later incorporated in the Radiotelegraph Convention, London (Article 17) and in the Montreux Convention (Article 2). It establishes the right of "the Members and Associates to keep the transmission of any particular telegram or to interrupt any other particular telecommunication that seems dangerous to the State security or [is] against its laws, public order or morals." The principle, with this limitation, constitutes the juridical basis of the international law of communications.

Another basic juridical principle, specific to radiotelegraphy, was established by the Conventions of Berlin, 1906 (Article 5), and London, 1912 (Article 8), stating that the operation of radiotelegraphic stations was organized, so far as possible, in such a way as not to interfere with the functioning of other stations on the air. (*"L'exploitation des stations radiotélégraphiques est organisée, autant que possible, de manière à ne pas troubler le service d'autres stations de l'espace."*)

This statement of the principle is weakened mainly by the phrase, "as far as possible". On the other hand, at the Conventions on Telecommunications as opposed to the Conventions on Radiotelegraphy, these principles appear with more vigor. Article 10 of the Washington Convention of 1927 states that all stations should be installed "in a way that will not cause any harmful interference to the communications or to the radioelectric services of other Members or Associates" (see Montreux, Article 48).

This principle applies not only to member states but also to recognized private enterprise duly authorized to maintain radiocommunication services. It is directly connected to the principle of international allocation of frequencies and the registration of frequency assignments. This principle appears, in highly sophisticated form, in the South American Agreement of Buenos Aires, 1935, revised in Rio de Janeiro, 1937 (Article 12), which prohibits the granting of any allocation when it disturbs any other services.

The Institut de Droit International in its Lausanne session of 1927, as a result of Professor Arrigo Cavaglieri's report and after the intervention of Professors Higgins, Neumeyer and Basdevant, approved a Resolution proclaiming the liberty of transmission of radio waves (Article 3). A majority of the members rejected an amendment proposed by Professor Neumeyer requiring such transmission not to cause harm (*"passage non nuisible"*). Instead, they established the duties of good neighborhood and the duty not to disturb the services of other states (Article 4). This Resolution established the international responsibility of the state which causes serious disturbance (*"un trouble grave"*) if it does not take measures to suspend broadcasts aimed to disturb public order of another state (Article 5).

We are now in the space age. In November 1957, when this era was beginning, I proposed at a session of the Tenth Conference of the Inter-American Bar Association, in Buenos Aires, the creation of a committee on interplanetary space law.

At the next, or eleventh, Conference of the Association, in Miami in 1959, I proposed several further resolutions including one "to declare that solar or interplanetary space, that is, the extra-atmospheric space now being explored by man, is immune from appropriation, and free, constituting 'res communes omnium Universi,' a common 'res' for all intelligent creatures of the universe." I also moved to "declare that the interplanetary space may be utilized only for peaceful purposes, its ample use being assured for all in the universe, individuals, associations, states and groups, of the earth and other planets and satellites, for navigation, *radio broadcasting* and all other technico-scientific activities of a non-aggressive nature."

At that time I also mentioned that the problem in complying with the *res communes omnium* principle is one of the *regulation* of *use* and *enjoyment,* quoting the text of Article 585, n. II, of the Civil Code of Chile, as written by Andrés Bello, to the effect that: "The use and enjoyment of the things which Nature made common to all men shall be determined between the individuals of one nation by the laws of the latter, *and between different nations by the International Law."*

The first problem of our work, therefore, is to determine whether there are rules of international law in force regarding radiocommunication in space and direct broadcasting via satellites.

When the Institut de Droit International debated the Legal Statute of Space and voted the Resolution of Brussels in 1963, it approved, by general agreement, the principle that all nations should make sure that space telecommunications conform to ITU regulations. They did so considering it impossible to deal separately with the subject of space telecommunications, since all modes of telecommunication utilize the same finite frequency spectrum. The Institute also acknowledged the efficient way in which ITU had been dealing with such matters as the distribution of frequencies for space and earth-space radio service (since 1959 at the Administrative Conference in Geneva, and at the 1963 Extraordinary Conference in Geneva), the revision of the tables of frequency distribution and the approval of several resolutions and recommendations.

The principle established by the Institute received full juridical confirmation in the Treaty on Principles Governing the Activities of States in the Exploration and Use of Outer Space, Including the Moon and Other Celestial Bodies, London, Moscow and Washington, 1967.

The International Space Charter embodied in this Treaty is correct in that it proclaims that space and celestial bodies are *res communes omnium,* but is weakened by its failure to *regulate their respective use.* The Treaty includes express rules for the incorporation in space activities of all instruments of international law in force, including the Charter of the United Nations, and thus must also adopt the International Conventions on Telecommunication as positive international law with regard to radiocommunication activities in space.

Article 3 of the Space Treaty of 1967 prescribes that: "States Parties to the Treaty shall carry on activities in the exploration and use of out-

141

er space, including the Moon and other celestial bodies, *in accordance with international law,* including the Charter of the United Nations, in the interest of maintaining international peace and security and promoting international co-operation and understanding." Article 13 proclaims that: *"The provisions of this Treaty shall apply to the activities of States Parties to the Treaty in the exploration and use of outer space,* including the Moon and other celestial bodies, whether such activities are carried on by a single State Party to the Treaty or jointly with other States, including cases where they are carried on within the framework of international intergovernmental organizations."

The 1967 Treaty has, therefore, I submit, extended to outer space the international law in force on earth, with such exceptions as are specified in the text of the Treaty.

This feature of the Treaty was inspired by the Resolution of the Institut de Droit International of Brussels, 1963, which stated that to areas not explicitly covered by the text the general international law, including the principles of the U.N. Charter, would apply.

Thus Intelsat, dominated by the United States; Orbita, directed by the Soviet Union; and Symphonie, projected by France and Germany, are subject to the terms of the 1967 Treaty and to the other rules of international law in force, including the International Conventions on Telecommunications, which were ratified by, among others, the United States, the Soviet Union and France.

The International Telecommunication Union thus acted properly in dealing with the distribution of space frequencies in 1959 and 1963 and enumerating, in Article 4 of the Montreux Convention, as an objective of the Union "telecommunication of *all kinds*" (i.e., including telecommunication via satellite).

According to Article 3 of the Space Treaty of 1967, the International Conventions on Telecommunications apply to space activities "in the interest of keeping peace and international security and of promoting international cooperation and understanding."

Other articles of the Space Treaty of 1967 reinforce this principle. Article 9 states: "In the exploration and use of outer space, including the Moon and other celestial bodies, States Parties to the Treaty shall be guided by the principle of cooperation and mutual assistance and shall conduct all their activities in outer space, including the Moon and other celestial bodies, with due regard to the corresponding interests of all other States Parties to the Treaty." Article 9 also stipulates that if a state has reason to believe that its space activity might interfere harmfully with activities of other states, it shall undertake appropriate international consultation before undertaking that activity. The text also permits any other state, aware of the purpose and/or consequences of that activity, to request consultation.

In short, in accordance with Article 3 of the Space Treaty of 1967, the international dispositions in force with regard to radiocommunications, as well as the respective conventions and conferences, interpreted as maintaining peace and security; promoting international cooperation, understanding and mutual assistance; and impeding activities that might lead to harmful interferences with interests of other states, should be applied to radiocommunications in space.

By the same logic the following juridical principles of the Telecommunication Convention (especially those enumerated in Sections 6 and 7), should be applied to space telecommunications:

1. The free and equal utilization of services of radiocommunication should be granted to all without discrimination (Montreux Convention, Article 31).
2. This right may be limited if it presents a danger to a state's security or if it is contrary to that state's public order or to its morals (Montreux Convention, Article 32).
3. Radiocommunication services should be exploited without harmful interference to communications or radiotelegraph services of other states, and the frequencies for such services should be distributed internationally (Montreux Convention, Article 48).
4. Space radiocommunication, especially via satellite, shall be processed in the interest of the maintenance of peace and in the interest of international cooperation and understanding, impeding any harmful interferences by one state in the activities of any other, leading, if necessary, to an international procedure of consultations (Space Treaty, 1967, Articles 3 and 9).

The *Fifth principle* is a Latin American one. It is the principle concerning the prohibition of transmitting false news and programs aimed at disturbing good international relations, offensive to national feelings of other countries, harmful to the organization and consolidation of the peace and contrary to the sovereignty and integrity of nations.

The South American Agreement on Radiocommunication signed in Buenos Aires, 1935 and revised in Rio de Janeiro, 1937, in Article 2 stipulated:

1. In the broadcasting of news of an international political character concerning contracting parties (especially news of a purely political character), the source of the information should be identified so that only news received from qualified sources and duly authorized would be broadcasted.
2. Broadcasting of news and comments that might disturb international good relations or offend the national feeling of other people should be avoided.
3. Propaganda against the sovereignty and integrity of nations should also be avoided.

This Article was indeed a remarkable anticipation of the principles contained in the Charter of the United Nations and in the Space Treaty of 1967.

It shall be noted, furthermore, that at the Inter-American Conference held at Buenos Aires in December 1936, two Resolutions were approved: (1) the Resolution on Broadcasting and Moral Disarmament, which recommended to the American countries the ratification of the Geneva Convention of November 23, 1936, on the use of broadcasting for the purpose of peace; and (2) the Resolution on Broadcasting in the Service of Peace, which recommended that themes relating to the scientific, intellectual and material benefits of peace and to the peaceful settlement of international controversies be included in programs.

An alarming problem today arises from the near prospect of direct broadcasting through satellites. Such broadcasting would permit the entry in every home on earth of radio and television programs transmitted from anywhere, whether from earth or space.

In August 1968, at the Conference of the United Nations on the Exploration and Peaceful Use of Outer Space, Pope Paul VI stressed the *necessity for due control* when he asked, if the free circulation of information entailed the propagation of false news; if transmission facilities became an instrument for ideological propaganda leading to the spread of subversion, the excitement of hatred, the maintenance of racial discrimination and the opposition of peoples and social classes rather than their union; who would not see that the recent marvelous discoveries of science had turned against man and had worked toward his misfortune rather than his happiness?

Fortunately there now exist, I suggest, rules of international law that do away with such abuses. These rules are those appearing in the already mentioned Articles and in the 1967 Space Treaty as well as in

144

the International Telecommunication Convention (Montreux, Article 32) and especially in the South American Agreement on Radio Communications (Article 2).

Here it is important to mention the Geneva Convention of September 23, 1936, on the Use of Broadcasting in the Service of Peace, ratified by Brazil and several other states. The Convention especially forbids all forms of propaganda, mentioned by Pope Paul VI, which are harmful to peace and to human welfare.

These existing international rules will have to be enforced with regard to any satellites in the Intelsat and Orbita systems that are equipped with transmission and reception stations and also to any other satellite systems that might function in the future. Accordingly, the provisions of the international conventions mentioned above, which forbid the use of telecommunication against a state's security, laws, public order and morals, against good international relations or for circulating false news, and also those provisions that call for the maintenance of peace and security and the promotion of international cooperation and understanding, shall apply.

If a state or the responsible international telecommunication satellite organization fails to fulfill such obligations, they might be held responsible. According to Article 6 of the Space Treaty of 1967, the state injured by such illegal programs would be able to request the application of procedures for the peaceful settlement of the conflict established by the Montreux Convention (Article 28). The procedures include arbitration (Annex 3 and additional Protocol), which is also sanctioned by the Geneva Convention (Article 7). The latter Convention looks to the successive peaceful procedures bilaterally agreed upon (for example, settlement by the International Court of Justice or the Arbitration Court of The Hague).

A very important juridical problem concerning telecommunication is that which refers to the so-called pirate broadcasting stations, which operate from ships or airplanes in coastal zones of states, but outside their territorial waters. Such activities are now very common in Western Europe.

Article 7 (1) of the General Regulations on Radio Communication, adopted in Geneva in 1959, states that "pirate broadcasting activities constitute *per se* a violation" of the 1959 instruments. It adds that "the establishment and use of broadcasting stations (sound broadcasting and television broadcasting stations) on board ships, aircraft or any other floating object outside national territories is prohibited."

145

The words *per se* were used in that text because any stations operating without authorization or license from any government and causing harmful interference are considered to be pirate.

The problem of pirate stations could also exist in space, although only perhaps in the remote future. In anticipation of that, and considering the complexity of a communication satellite, it would be advisable to alter the regulation to include pirate space stations.

We agree with Evensen in his Hague Academy lectures of 1966 that pirate space stations would constitute an *international crime,* like genocide, piracy at sea, traffic in women and narcotics and that it should be punished universally like these other international crimes.

Evensen quotes legislation promulgated by Sweden, Norway, Finland and Denmark, in June and July of 1962, defining and prescribing punishment for various crimes analogous to piracy. But these laws are still rather modest, for they foresee only acts practiced and having effect within those countries. Also modest is the European Agreement for the Prevention of Broadcasts Transmitted from Stations Outside National Territories of January 22, 1965, which defines the act of such transmissions as a crime and obliges states to punish it according to their domestic law (Article 2), but only when practiced by their respective nationals (Article 3).

What should be done to solve this matter is to prepare an international convention punishing piracy by radio, as is the case with regard to piracy in the air and on the sea. To this purpose, what should be done would be to take as a model—something that, regrettably, was not done by the European Agreement of 1965—the Conventions on Genocide of the United Nations of December 9, 1948, and the Convention on Narcotics of 1961.

Finally, the problem of the exploration being carried out by communication satellites should be examined.

It is obviously a public service of the highest universal interest. One purpose of those satellites is to create a "university of the world" by providing, via satellites, televised educational courses which will reach remote villages all around the globe.

The ideal juridical form of those satellites, owing to the commercial connotation of the enterprise, would be a public international organization or one with private participation.

The best solution for the economic and social development of such satellites would be to unite the various satellite organizations (Intelsat, Intersputnik and Symphonie) in a single organization. This goal is really the proclaimed intention of the various organizations themselves, since they, too, generally declare themselves open to membership by other states. As long as this goal cannot be reached in practice, however, it is necessary to ensure coordination between the activities of the three systems. The international organ best suited to that purpose, and to which these organizations should be subordinated, is the International Telecommunication Union (ITU), already established as a specialized agency of the United Nations.

But it is important that the organizing states of communication satellite systems be alerted soon to the fact that in making treaties under international law they are acting in the same quality as those that plan corresponding organizations within any country. These states must reaffirm their obligation to respect and accomplish their purposes in accord with the rules of international law now in force, including the U.N. Charter and various other conventions such as the Space Treaty of 1967, the International Conventions on Telecommunications and the Geneva Conventions of September 23, 1936. The mere fact that the exploration of space by communication satellites is being conducted according to an agreement between several or even many states does not mean that such states may ignore or act contrary to the rules of international law to which they are bound.

There are still other important obligations to which states that explore by means of communication satellites should be subjected. These obligations they owe to all humanity. In this sense the character given by the United States Communications Satellite Act of 1962 to the Communications Satellite Corporation (Comsat) as "a privately owned company for profit" with the character of a monopoly should be criticized. The *animus lucrandi* cannot be the aim of a universal organization dedicated to the welfare of humanity.

Although the Preamble of the Intelsat Interim Agreement of 1964 says that the aim is to establish "the most efficient and economical service possible consistent with the best and most equitable use of the radio spectrum," the text of the Agreement says nothing about minimum tariffs and a reasonable or indispensable profit, a limitation that should form the basis of all public utilities in any state's contemporary internal (municipal) law.

Minimum tariffs are even foreseen by the International Conventions on Telecommunication. It is enough to refer to Article 4 (2c) of the Montreux Convention of 1965, which states with regard to tariffs that there should be a "minimum level consistent with a service of good

147

quality and a healthy and independent administration."

Closely connected with the foregoing is the clause establishing that satellite communications services cannot be used, directly or indirectly, for any monopolistic or any other abusive activity. A recent event, the transmission via satellite of the World Cup football matches, has demonstrated the necessity of such a clause.

In conclusion, we may suggest that the statutory framework of the systems of communication via satellite must incorporate the following:

First, general rules of international law, including the Charter of the United Nations, and especially the Space Treaty of 1967 and the International Conventions on Telecommunications.

Second, the principles of the South American Conventions on Radio Communication, signed in Buenos Aires, 1935, and revised in Rio de Janeiro, 1937 (Article 2) and of the Inter-American Conference for the Consolidation of the Peace (Recommendations signed in Buenos Aires, December 21, 1936; Convention on Broadcasting and Moral Disarmament and the Use of Broadcasting in the Service of Peace).

Third, the principles of the International Convention of Geneva of September 23, 1936, for the use of broadcasting in the interest of the peace.

Fourth, clauses ensuring that the services shall be carried on for the public welfare, and with good quality, minimum rates and fair profit.

Fifth, a provision prohibiting any monopolistic or any other abusive activity of the service.

148

Chapter 11

DIRECT BROADCAST SATELLITES AND FREEDOM OF INFORMATION

by *Jean d'Arcy,* Paris and New York

Only a few years from now communication satellites that will allow direct broadcasting from the satellite to individual receiving sets will go into operation. Just a few weeks ago nearly a third of the human population was able to follow, minute by minute, the dramatic rescue of the American astronauts, for through satellites most of the world's radio and television stations and networks transmitted this report. Tomorrow or the day after governmental or private terrestrial intervention may no longer be necessary, so that millions of people, in spite of borders and national controls, will be able to receive images and sounds coming directly from space.

Such a technical success is a challenge to the international community. New structures, new laws and conventions, and a new international broadcasting practice have to be established in the coming years. The challenge is without precedent in the history of international relations. If it is not possible to face it in time, if states do not realize that a limit to national sovereignty is for the good of individuals, the danger exists of seeing a new instrument—with all its potential for increased freedom —contributing paradoxically to a new restriction on the free circulation of ideas and information. There is, however, hope that humanity, confronted with the new communications revolution, will realize that the rules and the structures which were suitable for the time of scarcity are no longer the ones needed in the times of abundance in communications that we are now entering.

Technical data

Some simple technical explanations are necessary here.

As everybody knows, there are at present two types of communications satellites, random and stationary. Satellites of the first type, like the American satellites Telstar (1962) and Relay (1963) or the Soviet Molniya satellites presently in service, circle the earth and need relatively complicated ground stations with orientable antennas to track the

149

satellite from its appearance at one horizon to its disappearance at the other. The duration of the satellite's passage and therefore the length of time that signals can be sent to and received from the satellite depends on the circumterrestrial orbit used; it ranges from a few minutes for Telstar to several hours for Molniya.

The stationary satellites, put in orbit at 36,000 kilometers above the equator, move at a speed corresponding to the rotation of the earth and thus appear fixed above the horizon. They do not need, as do the random satellites, complicated ground stations, since the antennas can be permanently pointed toward them. The satellites for the Intelsat system, which are presently in position over the Atlantic, Indian and Pacific Oceans and thus permit a worldwide communication network, are stationary satellites.

Three successive stages of growth are scheduled for this last type of satellite. In the present stage, called point-to-point, the satellite establishes communication between one ground station and one or more others. The signal sent by the satellite's transmitter is relatively weak and requires for its reception, 36,000 kilometers away, wide antennas and sophisticated receiving and amplifying installations.

At the next stage comes the so-called distribution satellite, when the signal sent will be strong enough to be received by small, less complicated ground stations with smaller antennas. These stations will not require the highly qualified technical staff of point-to-point satellites and will be relatively cheap, very likely about one hundred times less expensive than the present ones. From these community installations the signal received will be distributed to individual receiving sets either by a conventional ground broadcasting station or by cable.

The third stage will bring the direct broadcast satellite, when the signal sent will be strong enough to be received on the ground by individual receiving sets equipped with small antennas. Obviously everything here depends on the power of the transmitter and therefore on the source of power aboard the satellite. Very likely this type of satellite will only go into service when it is possible to use a nuclear source of energy aboard the satellite.

The question of a schedule for the introduction of distribution and broadcast satellites was the first raised by the Working Group on Direct Broadcast Satellites, established by the Committee on the Peaceful Uses of Outer Space of the United Nations General Assembly.

During its first session at New York in February 1969, it arrived at the following conclusions by unanimous vote.

150

First the Working Group concluded:

> Direct broadcast into community receivers could be close at hand: technology currently under development might allow this in the mid-1970's. Such a system is considered to be less expensive to launch than one intended for reception directly into peoples homes.

Again, the Working Group concluded:

> Direct broadcast of television into augmented home receivers could become feasible technologically as soon as 1975. However, the cost factors for both the earth and space segments of such a system are inhibiting factors... Therefore, it is most unlikely that this type of system will be ready for deployment on an operational basis until many years after the projected date of feasibility.

Finally, according to the Working Group:

> Direct broadcasting of television signals into existing, unaugmented home receivers on an operational basis is not foreseen for the period 1970-1985. This reflects the lack of technological means to transmit signals of sufficient strength from satellites.

The forecasts of the Working Group already seem in process of partial verification one or two years ahead of time. As a matter of fact, an agreement has recently been reached by the United States' National Aeronautics and Space Administration and the Indian government to place at India's disposal in 1973 a distribution satellite of the ATS-F type, which would make it possible to supply television directly to five thousand communities of the subcontinent. It is an experimental, pilot project which, from the technical point of view as well as from that of the programming (for education, development, improved methods of cultivation, birth control, etc.) will be of exceptional value and will permit a practical determination of what will be the future of broadcasting for the rest of the world.

The probable future practice

For now, in light of the first conclusions of the United Nations Working Group and in light of the studies done since then by international organizations such as the International Telecommunication Union, UNESCO and others, it seems that we can imagine in a fairly realistic way what the future could be. And in this field a sound appreciation of what is technically and politically possible and of what is not is more than ever necessary. It is not unusual, indeed, when these problems are broached to hear comments and questions which show more the imagination of their authors and their taste for science fiction than their real knowledge

151

of the facts. It is often a universe like George Orwell's or Aldous Huxley's, a universe of *1984* for 1985, a soft of bravest or worst of worlds that is discussed. Sometimes we hear about a global system of satellites controlling all the world's communications in all forms, imposing upon everybody the same programs that assert the supremacy of one culture and that unify the world in the most subtle way. On other occasion a new war of waves is foreseen, a new battle of different propagandas which have left the earth in order to settle in space and which try to impose from outside a nation's frontiers the "presence" of certain other nations through the television image.

The reality seems to be somewhat different, and it is necessary to "demystify" the question. First, probably few programs transmitted by satellites will be really worldwide—transmitted simultaneously toward the five continents at the same time by a unique world authority. Arthur C. Clarke, who is known to be the first person, and that as early as 1945, to forecast and to design the communication satellite, recently proposed that humanity adopt a single world time which does not consider day or night or the hour differences. This proposition will perhaps be adopted one day as a precise consequence of the existence of communication satellites. Before that, so long as it is not adopted, night and day, with their consequences for work and rest, will still govern our clocks and condition our television habits. There are few programs with worldwide interest which would justify a unique and centralized programming. What seems more likely, on the contrary, if technology and economy one day permit and make necessary direct broadcasting from satellites, is the institution of regional broadcasting organizations corresponding to continents, to cultures and common stages of development and to compatible time systems. It is also certain that television creates the event, and that when it reaches its real dimensions—which are continental and planetary, instead of being narrowly national as they are today because of a technical and temporary accident—more and more programs will justify broadcast by satellites. The recent installation of the Prince of Wales, broadcast throughout the world, normally a provincial event, is a recent example. But such broadcasts imply a community of culture and of interests which will be reflected in practice in different regional structures and not in a single worldwide structure.

Moreover, the results of the propaganda war conducted since the war by short-wave radio appear, in the end, to have been disappointing for those who have spent so much effort and money and an important part of this worldwide but limited natural resource, the radio frequency spectrum. To those who see the maintenance or the development of a natural or ideological "presence" throughout the world, it is usually answered that from all we know about reactions the listener normally finds nothing but the confirmation of his prejudices and already formed opinions; and it is only in time of crisis that "short waves"—to which war gave birth—have their real justification. More likely, the big powers, before carrying their antagonisms into space, before wasting this still more limited natural resource, the part of the frequency spectrum available for space communications, will carefully examine whether the stake with all its consequences warrants it. A decision to give their "overseas services" —usually governmental and distinct from the ones used for the national audience—access to the satellites would be, moreover, in opposition to the spirit, if not to the letter, of the Declaration of Legal Principles Concerning the Activities of States in the Exploration and Use of Outer Space, adopted unanimously by the United Nations General Assembly on December 13, 1963, as well as to the Space Treaty of 1967 prepared and unanimously approved by the General Assembly. The 1963 Declaration, and the Treaty as well, mention in their Preambles and declare applicable to space Resolution 110 of November 3, 1947, condemning "propaganda designed or likely to provoke or encourage any threat to the peace, breach of the peace, or act of aggression."

In any case, the spirit of mutual tolerance, of international discipline, of restriction and at the same time of respect for national sovereignties that has been demonstrated by the big powers in their space exploration and use for a number of years seems to be a clear demonstration of their determination not to transfer to outer space their national rivalries, and of their desire to take, each time, new initiatives only with the tacit or express consent of each other. It is reasonable to think that it will be the same with the communication satellites, especially because, as the United Nations Working Group points out, full international cooperation—therefore leaving out the struggle for influence—is technically necessary for the full development of broadcast satellites.

Finally, a more realistic view is also necessary on what this development would be. Everyone today agrees that the direct broadcast satellites will not suddenly appear in space but will rather be the late result of a progressive development of space technology and of economic and technical capacities for ground reception. Some even wonder if these satellites will really be needed in certain regions of the globe.

What we can expect, in fact, is as a first stage the launching fairly soon of distribution satellites intended to serve a limited number of com-

153

munity receiving installations. As pointed out by the United Nations Working Group, in this stage it would still be possible for governments to have, if they desire it, a substantial control over the reception of the broadcasts. The arrival of these satellites will lead, on the other hand, to the creation of regional or continental structures where the governments will gain, very likely through their national broadcasting organizations, a working knowledge of international cooperation in the field of programs. Such organizations exist already in Europe with Eurovision and Intervision.

Following the successive developments in power of the distribution satellites, in every country community receiving installations will multiply, along with all the necessary supplementary ground equipment— small automatic conventional transmitting stations or cable systems— for the distribution of programs.

Eventually the very number of these small community installations and the density of the distribution network may ensure, at least in the industrialized countries where this density will be very great, that no particular need for direct broadcasting satellites will be felt at the time when technically and economically they could be put into service. The switch from the distribution satellite to the direct broadcast satellite, in case the latter would be really useful—as for instance for countries in the process of development and with large land masses (Brazil, India, Indonesia) and without sufficient ground equipment—will take place, it seems, progressively and gradually, giving the states time to develop the international programming structures and the national receiving structures which will allow them to protect their interests. At the same time, as has already been the case for Eurovision and Intervision, international rules of mutual tolerance and good neighborliness will develop which will permit maximum advantage to be taken of the new instrument. It is only in extreme cases, which the pressure of national public opinions in any case renders more and more rare, that states will eventually use the ultimate weapon that technology and police controls give them: the jamming of the broadcasts and the interdiction of reception.

International structures and freedom of information

The time is therefore coming when radio and television programs will be received directly, across national borders, by relatively simple ground stations. The structures established fifty years ago, which since have permitted the development of radio and television, had a national basis.

Yet even then radio waves were ignoring borders, and organizations which could have had an international basis, at least for certain frequencies, might already have been established. But the times were not ready for it. With the conquest of the air, national sovereignties had just stretched from the ground to the atmosphere. The ether, as it was called then, had to be part of the national domain; telecommunications, heir to the royal postal systems, were a symbol too, an incarnation of sovereignty within the borders; and it seemed quite natural to regard radio as an extension of the telephone—a wireless telephone—and to put it under tight national jurisdiction. Today—with the satellite orbiting 36,000 kilometers above this blue and brown planet where only the white clouds draw limits; above this globe that, thanks to space television, we finally learn to see exactly as it is and not as we thought it was for thousands of years—what was only a discarded opportunity, an international structure or structures for broadcasting, becomes a necessity.

What form can we give these structures that will allow us to use the new instrument for improved circulation of ideas and information and at the same time guarantee to states that their main interests will not be affected? On this question the United Nations General Assembly has not yet taken a position, and only some very general principles applicable to space communications have been drawn from the Outer Space Treaty of 1967. This Treaty provides, among other things, for freedom of the use of outer space (Article 1), prohibition of any kind of national appropriation (Article 2), applicability of international law and of the U.N. Charter to outer space (Article 3), liability of states for any space activities under their jurisdiction (Article 6), necessity of international cooperation and consultation and of respect for the interests of other states in their space activities (Articles 9, 10, 11). Many provisions of the Treaty have their origins in earlier resolutions of the General Assembly and especially Resolutions 1721 (XVI) and 1962 (XVIII). Resolution 1721 refers, for example, specifically to communication satellites in specifying that "communication by means of satellites should be available to the nations of the world as soon as practicable on a global and non-discriminatory basis." It is the same for Resolution 1802 (XVIII), adopted shortly afterwards, which emphasizes "the importance of international cooperation to achieve effective satellite communications which will be available on a worldwide basis."

However, the General Assembly has never gone beyond these general principles and has never discussed, in particular, which form to give to a world satellite organization which would permit Resolutions

1721 and 1802 to be implemented. The fundamental decisions on this topic have actually been taken in the capitals of the member states but not in the United Nations, as has been the case for the establishment of the Intelsat system in 1964 and for the proposition for creating the Intersputnik system. If the Preamble of the Agreement Establishing Interim Arrangements for a Global Commercial Communications Satellite System (Intelsat) refers expressly to Resolution 1721; if it is the same also for the Intersputnik system; if the American delegation at the time of the Twentieth Session reported to the First Commission on the creation of Intelsat; if the proposition of creation of Intersputnik is embodied in two documents[1] addressed to the Secretary-General of the Organization; still the General Assembly in 1965 was content merely to note "with satisfaction the growing measure of cooperation among many member states in the peaceful exploration and use of Outer Space" (Resolution 2130 [XX]). And in 1966 and 1967, the General Assembly confined itself to commenting on "the cooperative space programmes in effect between many member states" and to recommending "such progress to the attention of others" (Resolutions 2223 [XXI] and 2260 [XXII]), without ever discussing the question of one or several international communications satellite organizations.

It is not yet possible to determine which policy will be followed by the General Assembly on this topic when the Committee on Peaceful Uses of Outer Space presents its conclusions from the report of its Working Group on Direct Broadcast Satellites. The first two reports[2] of the Working Group, for the February 1969 and July-August 1969 Sessions, do not discuss the question. None of the preliminary reports introduced by the member states for the Third Session of May 1970 mentioned it.

It is to be expected that in this field, too, the General Assembly will eventually follow the policy it has adopted so far in the matters of outer space legislation: the policy to recognize *a posteriori* rather than to prescribe *a priori*. It is this line of conduct which has already been followed for the two essential principles of freedom to use outer space and of prohibition of national appropriation. We find, for instance, at the Thirteenth Session many declarations of member states recognizing in this fashion, *a posteriori,* as for example Chile's declaration: "Neither the United States nor the USSR had asked for permission to launch its satellites and no government appeared to have protested"; or Sweden's

[1] Doc. A/6668 of May 10, 1967 and A/AC 105/46 of August 9, 1968.
[2] Docs. A/AC 105/51 and A/AC 105/66.

declaration: "No protests had been made by States against the flight of artificial satellites over their territory"; or Italy's declaration that "artificial satellites . . . flew over virtually all the territories of States without a single protest having been made." On the other hand, a resolution by the United Arab Republic at the same Session suggested that "the legal problems which might arise immediately in connexion with the exploration of space—for example such problems as the regulation of satellite launchings and traffic in space—should be dealt with promptly, by the establishment of a coordinated international programme for the formulation and supervision of such regulations"; but this suggestion has never been taken into consideration. Neither has a suggestion from Brazil at the Eighteenth Session that "the Declaration of Legal Principles Governing the Activities of States in the Exploration and Use of Outer Space should have provided for some form of international scrutiny of any communications system based on satellites."

If the General Assembly remains faithful to this pragmatic line of conduct, if with wisdom it would rather not decide now what structures should be established, then the member states themselves will, in the coming years, have to innovate prudently themselves. By a series of bilateral or multilateral agreements they will have to experiment for some years at the regional level, where the homogeneity of traditions or of cultures always allows for easier agreements. This type of initiative could thus give rise to international structures which could be later recognized and accepted by the community of nations for the management of the broadcasting satellites.

The worldwide experience of fifty years of broadcasting can be used as a basis for such regional efforts. The question of the relations between broadcasting and government is in fact one which, at a national level in the different countries in recent years, has been given maximum research and effort in order to bring about the best possible utilization of a communication instrument, the capacities of which have not been fully explored, for the individual as well as for the communities.

It is usual to contrast in these matters a type of structure called governmental and another one called commercial or independent. These two types of organization are actually much more similar than is usually admitted. Whether the ones in control are the states or private interests, a notion of primary liability of the station not toward the government, which in places nominates the people responsible, nor toward the advertisers, who in other places pay, but toward the public, which everywhere receives, has gradually emerged.

157

In a kind of struggle for liberation, not for a vain lonely autonomy in the midst of society but for a deeper commitment or a more important responsibility toward it, we have seen the broadcasters in both types of structures gradually establishing this notion of public interest as the essential reason for this choice of programs. As in the commercial type of structure, the state tends little by little to reinforce the powers of the central coordinating agency (FCC or others), and more and more gives it the responsibility to take care that the stations be really directed to the public interest. Likewise in the governmental type of structure for broadcasting, the governments progressively realize that it is in the interest of the nation and of themselves not to manage broadcasting directly but, for a better credibility and for a better defense of the general interest, to place between the antenna and themselves an organization fully responsible to public opinion. The evolution in this latter case has been obvious over the past fifty years, where—except for the BBC, an exemplary pioneer which came fully armed in the twenties—we have seen the national networks, in order to become more fully responsible, progressively gaining their autonomy from the PTT or Post Offices of which, in the beginning, they were only a department.

It would be paradoxical if these fifty years of experience at the national level were not turned to account at the international level and if in building new structures we fell again into the gropings of the beginning. Clearly, by Article 6 of the Space Treaty, states are liable for the space activities of their nationals and national agencies and therefore are directly and individually liable for space communications. Therefore they will be liable directly and individually for the radio and television programs transmitted from the direct broadcast satellites. To deduce from this that they themselves must directly control the transmitted programs would lead us again into the same mistakes of direct management made by some at the beginning of the broadcasting period. Such direct management will certainly lead, because of constant pressures, as contemporary examples prove, to programs without any interest, and also to new and very important restrictions on freedom of information and on the free circulation of ideas. That could be a big step backwards in the road to liberty of information opened in 1948 by the Universal Declaration of Human Rights, particularly Article 19.

In order to avoid the dangers of such direct management by the states, a possible solution would be to transpose to the international regional level what today exists at the national level after fifty years of progressive evolution of the structures. It would take the form of a two-tier structure. On the one hand, there would be an intergovernmental region-al agency as owner of the satellite, having only the technical control and management, corresponding to the ministerial departments respon-sible for telecommunications to be found in every government. On the other hand, there would be a non-governmental regional agency re-sponsible for the programs, corresponding to the broadcasting organi-zations in each country. The basis for the creation of such regional broadcasting agencies already exists in several areas of the world in the form of broadcasting associations or regional broadcasting unions. They can be found in Western Europe under the name of European Broadcast-ing Union (UER-EBU), in Eastern Europe under the name of Organi-sation Internationale de Radio et de Télévision (OIRT), in Asia as the Asian Broadcasting Union (ABU), and in Africa as the Union des Ra-dios et Télévisions Nationales Africaines (URTNA). These unions are associations of national broadcasting organizations; they manage com-mon material and laboratories and already have some experience in common programming, in the form of either program exchanges or ven-tures in coproduction or, more especially for UER-EBU and for OIRT, in the form of common networks such as Eurovision and Intervision, which themselves could very well be a model for these regional satellite broadcasting agencies that we have just discussed.

In the report of its Second Session[3] the United Nations Working Group has this to say about Eurovision and Intervision. In Paragraph 46 of the report, the Working Group notes that "the cooperation par-ticularly evident in the activities carried out by broadcasting organiza-tions in Europe under the name of Eurovision (EBU) and Inter-vision (OIRT), includes, among others, arrangements for live televi-sion programme exchanges as well as cooperation in some matters of common concern to the member organizations. The patterns which have grown up with Eurovision and Intervision for the use of terrestrial cir-cuits have already been extended to the use of communication satellite systems. The use of satellite systems for television has already made possible new patterns of cooperation between broadcasting organiza-tions in widely separated areas of the world and provides opportunities for extending regionally evolved cooperation to a broader international level."

In Paragraph 47, the Working Group goes on to note that "through such activities and arrangements carried out as the basis of voluntary common action, respecting the independence of each individual broad-

[3] Doc. A/AC 105/66.

casting organization, broadcasters have been able to solve a number of international problems in various areas. These include arrangements for harmonizing activities, joint programme presentation and production, the solution of language problems and differences in legal rules and technical standards."

In Paragraph 48, "the Working Group recognizes the role that broadcasting organizations are playing and can continue to play in the coordinated development of broadcasting via satellites."

The international experience gathered by Eurovision and Intervision during sixteen years of existence for the one and fourteen years for the other is precious and shows particularly that between professionals and between those responsible for broadcasting it is always possible to work out agreements. As they did not have to bind the national prestige every time nor constantly to defend the sovereignty of their states, as is the case for governmental representatives, and as they could take their decisions according to the audience they knew, and not according to governmental directives elaborated in the isolation of governmental offices, the people responsible for Eurovision and Intervision have been able to circulate across boundaries and throughout the whole of Western and Eastern Europe an international flow of images and sounds without, to our knowledge, any protestation having been made by governments. The rules of the game have always been ones of tolerance and mutual respect, excluding every aspect of national propaganda and every program which might have offended the others. Thus, if I may write here some personal memories, Spain gave up all transmissions of bull fights, France agreed voluntarily not to present programs of fashion and *haute couture,* Italy did not create programs which could have been interpreted as touristic propaganda. Rules of life have thus been laid down by daily practice and joint liability. At the Vienna Space Conference of 1968, the Indian delegate, Professor Vikhram Sarabhai, technical president of the Conference, in regard to the problem of spillover—the crossing of borders by broadcasts coming from satellites—answered that he was not very preoccupied by it and that he even wished that it would happen, for it will be soon necessary for the "states to live like neighbors." Thanks to another technical instrument—the microwave link and the coaxial cable—which has shaped the customs (as the direct broadcasting satellite will in the future) for the last fifteen years through Eurovision and Intervision, the European countries have learned how to live like neighbors. Their experiences are precious and may, perhaps, for a safer structural guarantee for the freedom of information, be extended pro-

160

gressively and carefully to the rest of the world, in successive regional experiments based on the notion, elaborated before, of a governmental organization for technical management and of a non-governmental program organization composed of the users of the satellite.

If the problem does not seem to raise special difficulties for Europe, Africa and Asia, where regional broadcasting unions that could serve as the basis of program organizations already exist, it may nevertheless raise some on the North and South American continents.

In North America, the existence in the United States of antitrust legislation which prohibits the networks from any associations and any common policy and the fact that Canada and the United States would have been the only members of such an organization have had the result that there is as yet no regional union. The three United States commercial networks plus National Educational Television, the National Association of Educational Broadcasters and the U.S. Information Agency are associated members and not full members of the UER-EBU, as is, in Canada, the CBC. Very likely this problem of the adaptation of the legal regime of American radio and television to the new techniques will have to be resolved by the Congress, as much for the satellites of the American continent as for the possible participation of North America in the broadcasts of other satellites.

In South America, where the multiplication of radio and television stations and a legislation especially aimed at avoiding governmental control over them have hindered, in some cases, the emergence of strong national organizations, there is again no regional broadcasting union like those on other continents. The only professional organization existing is the Asociación Interamericana de Radiodifusión (AIR), of which the North American networks are also members, but it has not yet undertaken activities similar to those of the other unions. It does not seem to be able to serve as a basis, in its present form, for a regional program agency for satellites, and it is likely that it would be necessary to create an entirely new non-governmental organization in Latin America. If we bear in mind that the satellites contemplated for the continent following the UNESCO surveys of 1968 and 1969 in Brazil and elsewhere will be above all educational satellites, it would probably be necessary to turn primarily to the universities to make up the non-governmental program agency, thus remaining faithful to the essential notion of an agency managed not directly by governments but by the users. It is sure that the satellites will bring into Latin America profound and necessary reforms of the broadcasting structures which, with some exceptions, are

161

not yet adapted to the present times; and that from these changes will emerge one day the practical possibility of an association between the broadcasters and the regional, non-governmental agency.

In communications matters the international community frequently turns toward the United Nations and its specialized agencies for an international structure which will guarantee free and impartial circulation of information. Thus we can often observe many international conferences about the information media suggesting, to quote only some of the resolutions, the creation of a World Press Agency, a World Broadcasting Organization, a United Nations Specialized Space Agency in charge of all space activities, a World Satellite Program Agency, and the like. Within the United Nations itself, as early as the first debates on outer space, such suggestions have been made. Thus at the Thirteenth Session, Chile and Italy asked that the United Nations control the use of outer space by member states, while Canada suggested that space activities be taken over by a United Nations specialized agency. At the Seventeenth Session Peru proposed that the United Nations receive the power to settle conflicts in space, Pakistan asked that the United Nations Secretary-General be appointed mediator for space problems and Austria suggested the creation of a world communications satellite system, while Brazil asserted that the satellite broadcasts of radio and television programs should be placed under the control of the U.N.

These suggestions—without the adoption of an official position by the two main space powers—were opposed in 1961 by those who, like Sweden, pointed out that it was not necessary to call on the United Nations to control a communication satellite system or who, like France, stated that it was out of the question to give the United Nations any kind of monopoly in the exploration and use of outer space or to impose on the member states a particular kind of cooperation, while in the following year Mexico reminded the member states that the United Nations was not a supergovernment.

Since the institution of Intelsat in 1964, the discussions on this topic have become less broad, but Intelsat, a governmental organization, is only a common carrier without any role in the field of programs. The debate may revive one day if the Intelsat members do not arrive at a definitive agreement or if the question of the control of programs is once again raised before the General Assembly. It is sure, however, that the control of information and of programs transmitted by satellites is one of the most critical questions, and there are many today who think that recourse to control by the United Nations or one of its specialized agencies is not, perhaps, the best solution. Such a control would always in fact be intergovernmental by nature. A United Nations Press Agency and a United Nations or UNESCO World Broadcasting Agency would be intergovernmental agencies. It would probably be impossible for many states to participate because of their constitutions. But if such agencies were established it is to be feared that the objectivity and impartiality that should be their aims would be reached only at the price of silence and constant self-censorship.

Such suggestions, generous and unselfish though they may be (and they usually come from the countries less favored with national information media, that is to say, those which need the most protection against a colonization of information), have their origins in an incomplete or inaccurate analysis of the possibilities of the world organization. Sometimes the promoters of these ideas unconsciously see the United Nations as an autonomous organization having its own life independent of the states which compose it and making its own decisions not according to the realities of day-to-day politics but according to high ideals of peace, justice and progress—a sort of technocratic world supergovernment. Or sometimes others argue that from the realistic opposition of national points of view comes a natural balance of objectivity and impartiality. The reality is unfortunately completely different. It seems that any direct governmental connection with information at the international level ought to be rejected for all the defensive protection of prestige and of sovereignty that it involves. And it seems incumbent upon the communications profession itself, with the help of the governments, to build the international structures that the new instruments call for and that the users need.

The two-tier type of structure—one governmental, the other non-governmental—could be a possible approach to explore. It seems, on the one hand, to give governments the guarantee that they would be able to exercise their responsibilities for their own nationals' activities according to Article 6 of the Space Treaty. On the other hand, it would permit space broadcasts to grow and to take on their true dimensions without constant governmental pressures. Such a solution, however, should not be imposed at the beginning by the General Assembly but should rather be recognized by it *a posteriori,* after a few years of experimentation region by region around the world.

163

Contents of the programs transmitted by satellites

It is obviously on this question that the attention of the member states has been concentrated. As early as 1962 suggestions were made to impose certain limitations on the contents of programs transmitted by satellites. A proposal by the Soviet Union that "the use of outer space for propagating war, national or racial hatred or enmity between nations shall be prohibited" has been supported by some countries. Brazil stated at the same session that "programmes transmitted by means of satellites should exclude all propaganda in favour of war, class struggle or racial or religious discrimination and propaganda likely to be offensive to another country." The United States did not support these two proposals. When, in 1963, the United States reached an agreement, negotiated directly with the Soviet Union, for the Declaration of Legal Principles Governing the Activities of States in the Exploration and Use of Outer Space (Resolution 1962 [XVIII]), a compromise noted above had been accepted to include in the Declaration's Preamble Resolution 110 (II) of November 3, 1947, "condemning propaganda designed or likely to provoke or encourage any threat to peace, breach of the peace or act of aggression."

It is to this question of the content of programs transmitted by satellites that the Working Group on Direct Broadcast Satellites has given the largest part of its Second Session report.[4] It considers the matter under four different titles: international legal aspects, political aspects, social and cultural aspects, and commercial aspects. Bound by the Space Committee's rule of "consensus," it does not give any conclusions but quotes the different regulations sought by some of its members in regard to interference in domestic affairs of states, incitement to racial or religious intolerance, war propaganda, incitement to social disorders, violation of fundamental human rights, and utilization of subliminal techniques. The report also points out the danger that satellite broadcasts could present in cases when "programmes ridiculed the beliefs of others or contained items involving obscenity, violence, or horror . . . or (would) emphasize inequalities of standards of living."

The report also points out that some delegations would like "to ban all commercial advertising from direct broadcast from satellites, the financial balance of the system being ensured by other means."

Thus the Working Group is extremely divided on what positive or restrictive approach to take about the contents of the programs. Para-

4 *Ibid.*

164

graph 22 says that "some delegations felt that freedom of the use of space and freedom of information in the field of satellite broadcasting should be qualified freedoms."

Two main proposals were made during this Session: first, the establishment of "a code of conduct, or of programme standards through international cooperation"; second, a rule of previous consent of a state to receive programs sent by satellites.

On the question of the code of conduct, the Working Group itself pointed out that "some scepticism was expressed, however, as to whether a generally acceptable code could be prepared and implemented, given differing views regarding, for example, freedom of speech, censorship and control of media." It seems indeed improbable, precisely because of the several stages of development throughout the world, that an agreement could be reached today on a universal code.

Neither has the Working Group been able to reach a consensus on the rule of previous consent. As the report notes, "Another suggestion was that it might be more consistent with generally accepted international law to put stress on the right of every State to refuse a satellite broadcast directed at its territory rather than to oblige those responsible for such a satellite system to seek the prior consent of each country likely to be covered by its broadcasts. Doubts were expressed, however, about the practicability of doing this."

To what extent can these two suggestions of the Working Group represent a workable solution to this new conflict between freedom of information and national sovereignty presented by direct broadcast satellites? It does seem that, little by little, states are coming to realize that, as has often happened in the past, the new tool will inevitably bring a reconsideration of past structures and that they will one day have to give up a new bastion of the fortress that historical developments, indeed relatively recent, had allowed them to erect around their borders.

On these grounds, certainly, "code" and "rule" are an attempt at temporary compromise by some states, which, because of the different stages of development of their societies as well as because of inadequacy of their information media, do not yet feel ready to open their borders completely. It is not the first time that the United Nations had dealt with the question of a code of conduct for the means of information. We remember that in May, 1950, the Subcommission on Information and the Press (established in 1947 by the Human Rights Commission) established a first draft of an international code. After it had been communicated to professional organizations, amended according to their remarks, and transmitted to the General Assembly, it was eventually dropped in 1954. It is feared that it will be the same for the code of conduct proposed today as a possible solution to the problem of direct broadcast satellites. If constitutional and legislative progress toward the freedom of information has been made in many countries, thus bringing about a more homogeneous situation throughout the world, certain states have nevertheless thought it necessary to tighten their controls. If, thanks especially to the efforts of UNESCO, ITU, and the UNPD, the last ten years have witnessed a spectacular development in the information media, particularly broadcasting, in countries which have recently acceded to independence, the situation has remained the same, however, in regard to international press agencies, for instance, which are still the attribute of major powers. The case of television is even more striking since the only worldwide agencies of television news are English-speaking. Therefore it is very likely that the Working Group on Direct Broadcast Satellites will not carry on the project for a code of conduct, at least not a worldwide code, but will rather leave the door open to a formulation by the information profession of codes corresponding to regional cultural and developmental stages. It may also simultaneously attempt to retreat to a "declaration of basic principles" such as the one suggested in December 1969 at the UNESCO meeting of governmental experts on international agreements in the field of space communications. But here, too, the Assembly remembers the experience of the past—the experience of the Draft Convention and of the Draft Declaration on the freedom of information. They have appeared on its agenda since, respectively, its Fourteenth and Fifteenth Sessions; the Preambles and four Articles in one and five in the other have been approved in Committee. Some of these articles could eventually be used for a "declaration of basic principles" for satellite broadcasting. But it seems wiser and, perhaps, more fruitful, rather than see the Working Group or the Legal Subcommittee of the Outer Space Committee make a detailed study that would probably repeat for several years the slow and difficult debates of the Third Commission, to suggest that the latter take up again the study of a declaration on the freedom of information in the light of the developments to come under the present revolution in communications.

Much of its work on this topic goes back to the Geneva Conference of March and April 1948 on the freedom of information, and it still bears the mark of the prewar period characterized by a dominant position of the printed media, themselves narrowly limited by national boundaries. The approaching advent of direct broadcast satellites and the

166

more and more obvious convergence of all media on electronics, with all its possibilities of individual, instantaneous, and cheap distribution regardless of distances, indeed give new dimensions to the problem of freedom of information that could not have been foreseen by the members of the 1948 Conference and their successors.

The second suggestion of the Working Group, the one on the rule of previous consent, represents an innovation in the field of broadcasting. Transposing into electromagnetic space the right of the states to bar the entry on their territory of certain publications and newspapers, it would have the advantage of endowing the states with a legal weapon they have lacked until now. They could use it as a negotiating tool when direct broadcasting systems are being introduced that otherwise might not have their participation. However, the text of the Working Group is not extremely clear on what the states would be able to accept or to refuse. After reading Paragraph 23 of the report,[5] however, we do not know whether it deals with a general, everlasting consent to broadcasts over the territory (sixth line: "prohibition of broadcasts beamed from satellites") or to program-by-program consent (fourteenth line: "the right of every State to refuse *a* satellite broadcast").

If the second interpretation is correct, it would probably seriously limit the development of direct broadcast satellites all over the world and would represent an exorbitant privilege given to states counter to their partners in a common venture, hindering them from enjoying common advantages peacefully and in good neighborhood. Moreover it would represent a possibility of direct and constant governmental intervention into information, and it would not finally stand up before public opinion. Such a rule would remind us, in fact, by its nature and because of the fear it shows of the new communication tools, of a step taken in London long ago that did not stand up either. If we believe Asa Briggs and his remarkable *History of Broadcasting in Great Britain,* at the very heroic beginning of radio the transmitting stations (the BBC was not yet there) had the right to transmit only for seven minutes. Then they had to stop for two minutes so that the Post Office could phone to say whether the program could go on for seven minutes more or whether it had to stop, purely and simply. At that time also the stations had the right to announce a news item only if the press had already published it. Today there is very little news which is published without having been broadcast here or there.

The present technology of directional antennas aboard satellites al-

[5] *Op. cit.* note 3.

167

lows for the transmission of beams as narrow as one degree and even less. Thus it would be possible one day to delimit on the surface of the earth areas of five hundred to one thousand kilometers with almost no variation of the synchronous satellite position. Therefore one can imagine that for large countries the rule of previous consent could be technically applicable. Thus the refusal of a single country would not prevent the neighboring countries from enjoying the benefits of the direct broadcast satellite. But for divided areas or continents—for Europe, for instance—the rule might, on the contrary, become excessive, giving to a single state the power in the name of its single national sovereignty to stop some twenty others in their common venture. Thus a rule good in principle might lead to an abuse. Moreover, it is possible that some states could not adhere to it because of their constitutions.

As a matter of fact, the rule which gives the states the equality weapon they need already potentially exists, but under another form. Their participation in the International Telecommunication Union secures this weapon for them. But the problem is, finally, the very one of ITU. Governments are mostly represented there, in fact, by their telecommunications organizations; and thus they do not feel that all the interests—other than the technical ones—they have to defend are completely represented. If a reform of ITU, long sought by some, comes about one day, it would probably result particularly in greater participation at the governmental level. The example of the long negotiations for the definitive agreement on Intelsat is, in this light, revealing. A governmental assembly is planned in the four-tier structure contemplated. It seems that the Working Group should assert, first, what is specifically cogent in its suggestion for previous consent: the right of every state to participate in discussions intended to establish a direct broadcast satellite system that would cover its territory. But next it should also draw immediate attention to the important role that ITU already plays, theoretically, through its IFRB, and will play in the future if a new role is recognized for it. This role is to be the guardian of a natural resource owned by mankind as a whole and no more by each particular state: the part of the radio frequency spectrum utilizable for direct broadcasting.

To finish with this question of consent, it is possible to imagine a regular procedure for protests and arbitration to give states an *a posteriori* appeal against programs that have reached their territories and that are regarded as harmful. Besides that, it would give the states a supplementary weapon to the ultimate one of jamming a satellite. Such a procedure would have the advantage of possibly leading to the institution

168

of a sort of international broadcasting court (or courts) of arbitration, the need for which will be felt more and more as satellites transmit sounds and images across borders. It is possible that the states' own public opinion, which as space broadcasting expands will press more and more for greater freedom in the information field, will limit their use of this procedure in practice, though it would always be a potential weapon. And thus states would learn progressively, as the distinguished Indian professor wished further back, "to live as neighbors."

Conclusion

The problems caused by the coming of direct broadcast satellites are reduced, in fact, to a re-examination of broadcasting structures, which have taken the narrowly national form we know, with their public or private local monopolies, only by a temporary historical accident of technological development. Broadcasting by its nature ignores borders, and in the end freedom of information can benefit greatly from the new instrument if we so desire.

The problem of spillover, even when intended, is not new. Without mentioning short-wave transmissions, how many radio stations have been built with the explicit or tacit previous consent of the neighboring states, precisely to reach these countries, without raising any major problems? Europe abounds with this kind of commercial station.

The difficulties met by the United Nations General Assembly on the way toward an international code of conduct for information media and toward a convention and a declaration on freedom of information are a clear lesson that we must proceed not on a universal scale but on a more modest, regional scale. There the homogeneity of traditions and cultures and the similar degrees of political, economic and social development allow neighboring states to trust each other in a common venture that, they know, will benefit their people.

It is not a series of prohibitions which will allow the development of these broadcasting satellites that everyone wants, but a positive approach to the problem—one relying on the professional experience gathered for fifteen years by the regional broadcasting organizations and finally leading to two-tier regional structures, the first governmental, the other non-governmental. What more or less evolved at the national level during the last fifty years to give every nation a telecommunication organization and a broadcasting organization is transposable to the international level for a better guarantee of freedom of information.

169

By giving telecommunications the strong world agency it needs—since today it is no longer primarily national as in 1865 but international— a better circulation of information will eventually emerge. For an ITU, too often a field of defense and of reciprocal neutralization of national sovereignties, must be gradually substituted an ITU really representative of the governments and a guardian of a common human patrimony.

When, finally, we think of the future facing us with its communications explosion, when we see the era of communications abundance we are entering after so many centuries of penury—some are still corresponding, at this very moment, somewhere in the world, by fire or smoke —and when we realize what is promised to us by the broadcast satellite, the microwave or coaxial cable for distribution of sounds and images and the recording of video cassettes, one cannot help thinking that it is not only broadcast structures but the very concept of communications that we will have to modify one day. What was justified by the times of penury—the public or private monopolies on communication—will no longer be justifiable tomorrow, when the access of everybody to what used to be the attributes of the rulers will be possible. We will have to speak not only of the right to information, as in Article 19 of the Universal Declaration of Human Rights, but of the human right to communication.